American Foreign Policy for the '80s

A Voter's Guide to the Facts and Issues

Prepared by the Editors of the Foreign Policy Association

New York, New York

1980

The Foreign Policy Association, which was founded in 1918, is a private, nonprofit, nonpartisan educational organization. Its objective is to help stimulate an informed, thoughtful, and articulate public opinion on foreign policy issues facing the nation. To this end it works closely with many public and private organizations and with colleges and schools. The Association strives to air diverse viewpoints impartially; it advocates none.

All rights reserved. No part of this book may be reproduced or transmitted in any form or by any means, electronic or mechanical, including photocopying, recording or by any information storage and retrieval system, without permission in writing from the Publisher.

Published by the Foreign Policy Association.
Editor, Wallace Irwin Jr.;
Managing Editor, Nancy L. Hoepli;
Associate Editors, Ann R. Monjo
and Gwen Crowe; Assistant Editor,
Christopher A. Kojm.
Design, Ann R. Monjo.
Cover, Hersch Wartik.

©Copyright 1980 by Foreign Policy Association, Inc., 205 Lexington Avenue, New York, N.Y. 10016.

Printed in the United States of America.

Library of Congress
Card Number: 80-66706.

ISBN 0-87124-060-2.

CONTENTS

Foreword 4

Leadership: President
vs. Congress 5

SECURITY
U.S. Defense Policy 12
International Terrorism 19

ECONOMIC ISSUES
Energy: U.S. Dependence
on Foreign Oil 26
Trade and the Dollar 33
The UN and Third-World
Development 40

AFRICA
Southern Africa 47

ASIA
China and Taiwan 54
Cambodia, Vietnam
and the Refugee Crisis 61

LATIN AMERICA
The Caribbean
and Central America 68

MIDDLE EAST
The Arab-Israeli Conflict 75
Iran, Afghanistan
and the Persian Gulf 82

U.S.S.R.
After Afghanistan:
The U.S. and Russia 89

FOREWORD

This is the fourth in a series of foreign policy background briefs produced for interested citizens by the Foreign Policy Association in each presidential election year since 1968. Its purpose is to provide voters, officeholders and candidates with enough background information on major foreign policy issues so that they can follow the debates and reach their own informed conclusions.

Many of the 13 topics covered in these pages have been prominent in early stages of the 1980 campaign. Others, less prominent now, are important in their own right and could become headline issues overnight. All of them seem certain to survive the 1980 campaign and confront President, Congress and nation in 1981 and thereafter.

The material is written in telegraphic style to get the essential information into a limited space. As in FPA's well-known annual **Great Decisions,** *from which much of the information here is drawn, the facts have been carefully researched and the approach is strictly impartial and nonpartisan. Each topic includes a section tracing Administration policy and concludes by presenting alternatives to present policy, with main arguments pro and con. A few additional readings are listed for each subject.*

Interested citizens, by their votes and voices, ultimately decide the course of U.S. foreign policy with all its great consequences. The editors hope this small book will enable more citizens to play their essential part more knowledgeably.

1

Leadership: President vs. Congress

- Do we need stronger presidential leadership?
- What is Congress' proper role in foreign policy?
- Who can best define the national interest — Congress or the President?
- Should there be more — or fewer — congressional curbs on the President?

ISSUE

Midway through Carter's first term, Senate Republicans criticized President's lack of leadership and issued a manifesto charging him with "incoherence, inconsistency and ineptitude" in setting foreign policy and national security objectives. President, in turn, blamed Congress for restricting his authority and interfering with conduct of foreign affairs. Public, according to polls, had declining opinion of both President and Congress, with confidence in Congress well below confidence in presidential leadership. Respected London-based International Institute for Strategic Studies divided blame: White House for often lacking centralized means of translating differences of opinion into coherent policy; Congress for adding uncertainty to U.S. position by quarreling with President, becoming involved in setting policy, thereby causing fragmentation in decision-making.

Seizure of U.S. Embassy staff in Teheran, Iran, on Nov. 4 and Soviet invasion of Afghanistan Dec. 1979 temporarily stilled attacks on Carter as lacking leadership. Public and Congress, as in other times of national crisis, rallied behind their President. Even rival presidential candidates temporarily muted criticism. But charges against President — incompetence, too little or too much action — soon resurfaced with new events; and similar charges leveled against Congress. If country has shed "Vietnam syndrome" and is now prepared to play more assertive, even interventionist role abroad, is it also ready for return to "imperial presidency"? If greater congressional checks on President's foreign policy powers are desirable, is country willing to accept increased risk of inept, rash or inadequate action by Congress?

BACKGROUND

■ **Fragmentation** in foreign policy-making is as old as Constitution. Founding Fathers named President Commander-in-Chief and gave him power, "by and with the advice and consent of the Senate," to make treaties and appoint ambassadors and other officers. They gave Congress power to "provide for the common defense," regulate foreign trade, declare war, raise and support armies and a navy. Expenditures for foreign aid, energy development are also subject to Congress' "power of the purse" — authorization and (separately) annual appropriation. Constitution gives Congress exclusive power to declare war but it neither explicitly grants Congress power to send troops abroad nor does it deny such authority to President. Constitution, in short, "is an invitation to struggle for the privilege of directing U.S. foreign policy."

Struggle has seesawed between legislative and Executive branches. For most of this century, presidential government, with center of power in White House, predominated, culminating in "imperial presidency": President Lyndon Johnson was criticized for usurping Congress' power to declare war; President Nixon for broadening and institutionalizing war-making power, denying Congress information, abusing Executive agreements to circumvent Senate's treaty power, impounding (refusing to spend) funds appropriated for projects he opposed.

Congress, in wake of <u>anti-Vietnam backlash</u> beginning 1968, sought to redress balance by restricting President's power to (1) commit troops without consulting Congress (1969 National Commitments Resolution and 1973 War Powers Resolution, latter passed over Nixon veto), (2) sustain military operations, (3) circumvent Congress by substituting Executive agreements for treaties (Case Act of 1972), (4) order covert actions by CIA (Hughes-Ryan Amendment of 1974 requiring President to inform "appropriate" congressional committees).

Congress became even more assertive as result of Watergate scandal and Nixon resignation in Aug. 1974 and as post-Pearl Harbor generation, who deferred to strong Executive, left Congress. More than half Representatives in House in 1980 elected since 1972. Greater number of members interested in foreign policy, less deferential to views of foreign affairs committees. They have more access to intelligence data, travel more, have stronger professional staffs. Examples of assertiveness:

▶ 1974 Congressional Budget and Impoundment Control Act, which strengthens Congress' role in determining budget policies, priorities;

▶ Jackson-Vanik Amendment to 1974 Trade Act linking trade concessions for U.S.S.R., other Communist nations to freer emigration of Soviet Jews and others;

▶ suspension of military aid to Turkey voted in 1974 after Turkey's intervention in Cyprus (repealed in 1978);

▶ 1975 Clark Amendment cutting off U.S. covert aid to anti-Marxist factions in Angola;

▶ 1976 Symington Amendment to International Security Assistance Act barring economic aid to countries using nuclear reprocessing facilities without setting up international safeguards (e.g. Pakistan); and another amendment to same law requiring Executive to inform Congress 30 days before sale of military equipment worth more than $7 million;

▶ forced modification of fighter-plane package deal for Egypt, Israel, Saudi Arabia in spring 1979 (Congress threatened "legislative veto").

Congress also prohibited aid to countries found guilty of gross human rights violations, countries with socialist governments, etc. Afghanistan in Oct. 1979 became 26th such country. Moves to tie similar strings to aid channeled through UN and international lending agencies ultimately defeated.

Has Congress gone too far in curbing President?
Administration has protested that measures such as Jackson-Vanik, Turkish arms embargo, amendment of Mideast arms package interfered in foreign policy-making. Jackson-Vanik deprived President of bargaining chips in negotiating with Russians; Turkish arms embargo weakened NATO's southern flank; revision of Mideast arms package threatened delicate Mideast peace settlement. In this view, Congress should stop running foreign policy.

Charges of congressional interference, others claim, are exaggerated: on balance, Congress has used powers more as ally than as foe of Administration. On major issues — Panama Canal treaties, arms sales, normalization of relations with China, repeal of Turkish arms embargo, sanctions against Rhodesia — Administration eventually got most of what it wanted. Problem is not too much congressional constraint but not enough, according to this view. In crunch, Carter, like his predecessors, acted without consulting Congress, e.g., provided U.S. airlift of foreign troops to Shaba (Zaire) in 1978; sent arms, advisers to North Yemen in 1979; sent naval task force in 1979 and 1,800 Marines in 1980 to Arabian sea. Congress, by not objecting, invited further abuse of legal curbs on President.

ALTERNATIVES TO PRESENT POLICY

■ **Maintain and increase present congressional curbs on President's foreign policy prerogatives.**
Pro: (1) An imperial President, out of touch with national constituency, is greater threat than Congress whose slow deliberations often prevent headstrong, unwise presidential action.

(2) Curbs on presidency are necessary to prevent bureaucratic arrogance, more disasters like Vietnam — especially as calls for U.S. intervention abroad arise again. **(3)** Curbs reflect continuing public distrust of every President since Vietnam war. **(4)** Because Congress mirrors great diversity of opinion and interests across U.S., its participation necessary to legitimize foreign policy, gain indispensable public support. **(5)** Restrictions are not crippling. In times of crisis, Congress and country always rally round the President.

Con: **(1)** Only single Executive can speak and act promptly and coherently on vital U.S. interests. Divided authority sows confusion, undermines U.S. world leadership. **(2)** As Chief Executive and Commander-in-Chief, President alone commands necessary administrative machinery and expert knowledge. **(3)** Unlike Congress, President has national constituency, can resist local and special-interest pressures. Congress, its 535 members each immersed in own local interests, is incapable of coherent foreign policy; wastes time on details, neglects vital legislation; low public esteem well deserved. **(4)** Strong presidency need not be "imperial"; can respect Constitution, consult Congress as needed.

■ **Strengthen both President and Congress in their foreign policy roles.**

Pro: **(1)** Issue isn't whether Congress or President should be stronger, but how both can "be strengthened to do pressing work that falls to each to do, and to both to do together" (Dean Acheson, Secretary of State, 1949-52). **(2)** President can help by improving consultation. **(3)** Congress can strengthen President by better performance on vital legislation—and by leaving execution of policy, once formulated through consultation, to him. **(4)** Voter can strengthen both by demanding wider "national" view of foreign policy.

Con: **(1)** Division of power between Executive and legislative branches may be a luxury U.S. can no longer afford (former Secretary of Treasury C. Douglas Dillon). **(2)** When country can be destroyed at push of a button, only President should be empowered to make life-and-death decisions affecting its defense: congressional demand for consultation must yield to reality. **(3)** We don't need stronger President *or* stronger Congress but more realistic understanding of limits of power of both and of the country as a whole.

Select Bibliography

Fulbright, J. William, "The Legislator as Educator." Foreign Affairs, *Spring 1979. $3.00.*

Hamilton, Lee H. and Van Dusen, Michael H., "Making Separation of Powers Work." Foreign Affairs, *Fall 1978. $3.00.*

Tolchin, Martin, "Congress Broadens Its Influence on Foreign Policy." The New York Times, *Dec. 24, 1979.*

2

U.S. Defense Policy

- Are we spending enough on defense?
- What future for the nuclear balance and arms control?
- What should be the top U.S. defense budget priorities?
- Should Selective Service registration — and perhaps the draft — be restored?

BACKGROUND

Defense budget. In aftermath of Vietnam, U.S. underwent rapid demobilization. Inflation also cut into budget. Only in 1977 did U.S. defense budget begin increase in constant dollars.

Soviet Union steadily increased real military spending during same period 3-4% annually. De-

U.S.-Soviet Military Comparisons

	Spending (1976 constant $bil.) U.S.	U.S.S.R.	% of GNP U.S.	U.S.S.R.	Manpower (thousands) U.S.	U.S.S.R.
1968	130	101	9.5	11-13	3,547	3,220
1972	104	113	6.8	11-13	2,391	3,375
1976	91	130	5.4	11-14	2,087	3,650
1978	99	134	5.0	11-14	2,069	3,638

spite GNP only half as large, Soviet Union has outspent U.S. by at least $100 billion in past decade.

Strategic forces. Soviets have increased both number and accuracy of nuclear warheads. Analysts calculate that by mid-1980s Soviets will possess theoretical capability to destroy U.S. land-based ICBMs in "first strike," which may give them powerful leverage over U.S. in crisis confrontations.

Other analysts believe that first-strike notion is meaningless. A nuclear balance does not deter nuclear weapons use; threat of nuclear war itself does. Whatever supposed advantages of first strike, consequences of nuclear war are grave and unknowable.

U.S.-Soviet Nuclear Forces

	U.S.	U.S.S.R.
All Strategic Weapons	2,075	2,504
Land-based ICBMs	1,054	1,398
SLBMs	656	950
Strategic Bombers	365	156
Total Nuclear Warheads	9,200	5,000

Theater nuclear weapons. New Soviet weapons targeted on European cities and NATO installations include Soviet Backfire bomber (which may also have capability for one-way strategic mission against U.S.) and highly accurate triple-warhead, land-mobile missile known as SS-20. Over 900 Soviet weapons systems targeted on Western Europe; NATO has little countervailing missile force.

Conventional forces. U.S. Army of 208,000 in West Germany a visible presence to deter Soviet attack. In "third world," U.S. since early 1970s relied on Nixon Doctrine — that local regimes, supplied with U.S. weapons, would provide own security and protect American interests. But fall of shah of Iran raised question anew, for first time since Vietnam, of role of U.S. force in "third world."

Number of ships in U.S. Navy declined in two decades, from 955 to 458. Because of high technology and power of 13 aircraft carriers, U.S. still controls seas. But Soviet navy improved greatly: no longer just coastal defense force.

Draft. President Nixon ended military draft in 1973; Selective Service registration ended in 1975. Manpower costs of all-volunteer force high: 60% of U.S. defense budget versus 30% in Soviet Union. Also decreasing manpower pool. In 1978 2.1 million men reached age 18, but in 1985 figure will drop to 1.8 million. In 1979 recruiting shortfalls for first time in all four military services. National Guard and Reserve 150,000 below strength. Individual Ready Reserve of trained personnel half million below required strength of 700,000.

At same time, many defenders of all-volunteer army. Morale high, troops motivated. Drug problems, violence and racial tensions down sharply.

CARTER ADMINISTRATION POLICY

Defense budget. To counter growing Soviet military power, Carter Administration pledged in 1977 3% annual increase in real defense spending — strong commitment, given that most expenditures in Federal budget holding steady or declining in real terms. Because of hostage crisis in Iran, shock of Soviet invasion of Afghanistan, Carter asked for real boost of 5.4% in FY 1981, a sizable spending increase of $15.8 billion. New political climate favors defense spending. 1971 Harris survey found only 11% in favor of increased defense spending; 1979 poll found 60% in favor. But how should U.S. spend added dollars?

Strategic forces. President Carter, in inaugural address, hoped to move toward "elimination of all nuclear weapons from this earth." SALT II signed by Carter and Brezhnev in June 1979 far more modest achievement. SALT II established missile-launcher ceiling at 2,400, with provision for modest reduction to 2,250. Treaty also placed ceiling of 1,320 on launchers with multiple warheads, and ceiling of 10 on number of warheads per ICBM.

Although summer 1979 hearings generally favorable to treaty, SALT II faced difficult ratification fight in U.S. Senate. Discovery of Soviet combat troops in Cuba in Aug. 1979, Nov. seizure of American hostages in Iran led to delays in Senate consideration. Finally, Soviet invasion of Afghanistan Dec. 24, 1979 doomed treaty; caused Carter to withdraw it from consideration, almost certainly until after 1980 elections, if ever.

If SALT II killed, many treaty supporters believe all restraints on arms race will end. Some SALT II opponents favor this. Treaty rejection will demonstrate U.S. "resolve" in dealing with Soviets; U.S. military production can outstrip any Soviet efforts. The Committee on the Present Danger would like to see: (1) new bomber to replace canceled B-1; (2) accelerated Trident submarine program; (3) rehabilitated U.S. air defense program.

If SALT II ratified, arms control future equally cloudy. Treaty only defines rules of arms race; does not stop it. For serious chance of SALT ratification, Administration had to approve massive $33 billion 10-year program for land-mobile MX ICBM, designed to answer problem of U.S. ICBM vulnerability.

European nuclear balance. To counter Soviet weapons, Carter Administration sought and won NATO approval in Dec. 1979 of $5 billion plan to replace 572 tactical nuclear weapons with new 1,000-mile-range missiles in Britain, West Germany, Italy and possibly Belgium and the Netherlands. For first time, U.S. missiles in Europe would be capable of hitting targets in western U.S.S.R.

NATO approved new nuclear weapons in hope they would provide sufficient incentive for Soviets to negotiate limiting deployment of their own Europe-targeted weapons. But no negotiations on arms limits thus far, which in any case are predicated on SALT II ratification.

Conventional forces. Chairman of the Joint Chiefs of Staff General David C. Jones believes strategic programs fully funded; would like to see increased spending on conventional programs, including mundane things such as more spare parts, training, ammunition, repair and maintenance.

Carter Administration devoted first 2 years to strengthening NATO. But Iran, Afghanistan crises shifted 1980 attention to Persian Gulf, creation of 110,000-man Rapid Deployment Force and Indian Ocean fleet.

Administration's FY 1981 emphasis on air- and sea-lift capacity. At present, would take about month to send 15,000 troops and equipment to Persian Gulf; plan by mid-1980s to be ready to send full 110,000 force within 3 weeks. Administration also plans to increase fleet to 550 ships by 1990s.

Selective Service. Crises of 1979 also caused Administration in Jan. 1980 to reverse stance of previous 3 years and ask Congress for renewed Selective Service registration. Under Administration plan, 19- and 20-year-olds — both men and women — would be required to register.

ALTERNATIVES TO PRESENT POLICY

■ **Increase military spending.**

Pro: (1) First priority must be to match Soviet defense spending, deter Soviet aggression. If that fails, other priorities do not matter. (2) Allies will not increase defense spending if we do not lead way. (3) Defense spending at all-time post-World War II low as percentage of GNP. Increase not unreasonable burden.

Con: (1) U.S. and Soviet military budgets not comparable. U.S. has only one major adversary, while Soviet Union faces Western Europe, Japan and China as well as U.S. (2) Increased defense spending can decrease national security; cause arms spiral. Will encourage military solutions to political problems. (3) More for defense means less for social welfare.

■ **Pursue ratification of Salt II; pursue future arms control agreements.**

Pro: (1) SALT II is in national interest; not favor to anyone except ourselves. To block arms control contributes to arms race. (2) SALT useful political process; helps stabilize superpower relations.

Con: (1) We should stop arms control negotiations until we better define our defense needs. (2) Arms control an illusion; only ratifies Soviet military buildup. Has lulled us into neglecting our defense.

■ Use added defense dollars for conventional forces rather than new strategic systems.

Pro: (1) Maintenance of bases, equipment and training most cost-effective way to improve U.S. preparedness. (2) MX and Trident programs already funded; other new strategic systems of questionable benefit given cost. (3) Rapid Deployment Force, Indian Ocean fleet should have higher priority to avoid dangerous reliance on quick use of nuclear weapons.

Con: (1) Strategic balance most important indicator of overall U.S.-Soviet military balance. (2) Greatest security danger is potential vulnerability of U.S. land-based ICBMs in 1980s. Necessary to reduce this period of vulnerability to avoid political blackmail by Soviet Union. (3) Rapid Deployment Force makes U.S. foreign adventure more likely. This could trigger strategic confrontation for which U.S. is unprepared.

(continued on page 96)

3

International Terrorism

- How can we combat international terrorism?
- Can we protect our diplomats against blackmail, kidnapping, assassination?
- Are we dealing with a new form of warfare?
- Is terrorism ever justified?

BACKGROUND

There is little agreement about precise definition of terrorism or terrorists. As cliché goes, "One man's freedom fighter is another man's terrorist." Terrorism can be seen as criminal behavior or revolutionary activity, but of a special kind: the deliberate use of violence or threats of violence against innocent people with intent to produce fear for political ends. It can be used by individuals or groups to dramatize political cause, obtain release of fellow terrorists, secure funds. Can also be seen as form of low-budget warfare. Some analysts widen definition to include lawless violence by regimes in power against political opposition.

Terrorism is not new phenomenon. Movements using terrorist tactics include nihilists in Czarist Russia; partisan movements in Hitler-occupied Europe during World War II; national liberation struggles in European colonies after war.

Terrorism used today by 2 types of groups (though some hard to classify): (1) Nationalist "freedom fighters" — ethnic, religious, linguistic groups — with clear, limited objectives such as unification of Ireland; Palestinian homeland; independence for Namibia (South-West Africa) or Puerto Rico; breakup of multi-ethnic Indonesia, Yugoslavia, Canada; autonomy for Kurds, Azerbaijanis, Basques. Supporters and sympathizers often number many thousands. Some groups gain wide international backing; may use other means (conventional war, diplomacy) besides terrorism. May eventually come to power. (2) Small, violent ideological groups (e.g. Japanese Red Army, Italy's Red Brigades), with little or no clear program, whose aim is mainly to destroy or destabilize existing institutions and whose sole weapon is terrorism. They may be far left or far right — self-styled Marxist-Leninists, Maoists, Fascists, anarchists, religious zealots. Some observers expect increased use of both groups by governments in "surrogate" (proxy) warfare against foreign adversaries.

Present generation of terrorists has advantages over past: (1) great international mobility and rapid communication; (2) command of instant global audience through electronic media; (3) sophisticated weaponry such as antitank rockets, portable ground-to-air missiles; (4) international underground network which helps train, supply, finance and provide sanctuaries for terrorists. Network believed to extend from Havana to Tripoli, Paris to Prague, Moscow to Lebanon and Southern Yemen. Believed to be increasingly linked to organized crime, international narcotics smuggling.

The record. Because of fear it instills, terrorism has an impact disproportionate to number engaged in it. By some accounts, actual number of international terrorists — other than nationalist "freedom fighters" — is no more than 3,000. Over 11-year period (1968-78) they were responsible for 3,000 incidents, 2,000 dead, 5,000 wounded. Of 3,000 attacks documented by CIA, 1,270 were directed at U.S. citizens or property. Most prevalent acts were bombings (2,000), kidnappings or hostage-taking (240), assassinations (200), armed attacks (160) and hijackings (90). Western Europe led with highest percentage of incidents — 37%; Latin America followed with 27%.

Most notorious recent acts of terrorism include:

▶ Seizure of diplomats at Dominican Republic Embassy in Bogotá, Colombia, Feb. 27, 1980 by urban guerrillas demanding $50 million ransom, release of 300 political prisoners.

▶ Take-over of Grand Mosque in Mecca Nov. 20, 1979 by 500 religious zealots calling for overthrow of Saudi Arabian monarchy.

▶ Seizure of hostages in U.S. Embassy in Teheran, Iran, Nov. 4, 1979 by Muslim militants demanding return of shah. This is first terrorist attack on diplomats condoned by host government.

▶ Assassination of Earl Mountbatten of Burma, cousin of Britain's Queen Elizabeth, by Provisional Irish Republican Army in Aug. 1979.

▶ Kidnapping of U.S. Ambassador to Afghanistan

Adolph Dubs by Muslim extremists Feb. 1979. Dubs killed in rescue attempt.

▶ Kidnapping and murder of Aldo Moro in May 1978 in Italy by Red Brigades.

In Turkey, terrorists claimed 100 lives a month in first half of 1979. In Spain, Basque terrorist group ETA responsible for more than 80 deaths in 1979. IRA and Protestant foes continue mutual terror in British-ruled Northern Ireland. In West Germany, no major terrorist act since 1977. But in Italy, kidnappings, bombings, shootings, after 1978 decline, increasing again.

In Latin America, terrorism has diminished since 1974. Many important groups of right and left, active a decade ago, have been suppressed or forced into exile — especially in Argentina, Chile, Bolivia, Peru, Uruguay. Terrorism still widespread in El Salvador; Puerto Rican Armed Forces of National Liberation (FALN) active on island and U.S. mainland. At opposite political pole, right-wing Pinochet government in Chile charged with murder of exiled former ambassador to U.S. Orlando Letelier, Washington, D.C., 1976; anti-Castro Cubans in U.S. bomb to publicize cause.

In Middle East, Palestinian Arabs continue sporadic terrorist attacks against Israelis; Israel counterattacks PLO base areas in Lebanon.

Measures to curb terrorism:
◆ *Hijacking:* 1963 Tokyo Convention requiring countries to return hijacked plane, passengers, crew; 1970 Hague and 1971 Montreal conventions proscribing any kind of sabotage of commercial aviation and requiring prosecution or extradition

of offenders (more than 100 countries have adhered); 1978 Bonn Declaration on Hijacking in which leaders of 7 largest industrial democracies agreed to suspend air traffic to and from country refusing to prosecute or return hijackers and/or aircraft promptly. These measures have resulted in significant decline in number of hijackings.

◆ *Diplomats:* 1973 New York Convention on Protection of Diplomats; entered into force in 1977.

◆ *Hostages:* Convention outlawing taking of hostages, considered by many single most important measure adopted by UN General Assembly in 1979. Signatories must prosecute hostage-takers or extradite them "without exception whatsoever." (Not yet in force early 1980.)

General Assembly in 1979 also adopted nonbinding resolution on measures to prevent international terrorism. Included call for study of "causes," implying grievances justify terrorism; so U.S., other Western countries abstained.

CARTER ADMINISTRATION POLICY

U.S. policy has two aspects: prevention and response. Prevention includes (1) eliminating political grievances which spawn terrorism (e.g. Mideast and Southern Africa peace efforts); (2) improved intelligence, including international exchange of information; (3) tightened security. Responses include (1) no-government-concessions policy (condemn all terrorist acts as criminal, make no concessions to blackmail, neither pay or negotiate ransom nor release prisoners); (2) improved interagency coordination in responding to terrorism. State Department maintains 24-hour Operations Center.

Iran hostages. U.S. at outset condemned seizure of U.S. Embassy as violation of international law; ruled out extradition of shah. Stated U.S. would not yield to international terrorism or blackmail. Retaliated with series of measured responses (see Issue No. 12).

Legislation to combat terrorism pending in Congress. Would impose sanctions on countries President determines show "pattern of support" for terrorism; would also require addition of "taggants" (oxide compounds) to explosive materials to aid in detection and identification. Opponents include gun lobby, chemical manufacturers.

ALTERNATIVES TO PRESENT POLICY
■ **Strengthen U.S. counterterrorist capability.**
Pro: Terrorism thrives when neglected or met with appeasement. Only decisive crackdown can halt it. Measures could include U.S. strike force to respond to terrorist acts; use of clandestine intelligence agents; mandatory death penalty for terrorists; curbs on terrorist arms traffic, e.g. requiring manufacturers of explosives to add taggants. Worldwide terrorist epidemic, unchecked, may herald collapse of Western civilization.
Con: Indiscriminate crackdown could degenerate into violence unworthy of a democracy; would play into terrorists' hands since they deliberately try to provoke repression so as to fan revolutionary anger, hasten collapse of authority. Any intelligence apparatus massive enough to detect all potential acts of terror-

ism would be incompatible with free, open society. Death penalty is not deterrent to terrorist who is prepared to kill and be killed. Sanctions are only effective when other countries support them. Curbs on arms traffic are burdensome, easily evaded, unlikely to aid law enforcement.

■ **Tolerate terrorism if the cause is just.**
Pro: Where there is no other remedy for an intolerable situation, terrorism may be justified as lesser evil: for example, against oppressive dictatorship or foreign occupation. For the weak and oppressed, terrorism may be their only weapon and only defense.
Con: Terrorism is always immoral and unjust. There can be no justification for deliberate killing of innocent people. Terrorism violates a universal human right—the right to bodily security and integrity.

Select Bibliography

"International Terrorism: 'Do Something! —But What?'" "Great Decisions '79. New York, Foreign Policy Association, 1979. $5.00.

Quainton, Anthony C.E., "Terrorism: Do Something! But What?" Department of State Bulletin, *Sept. 1979. $1.40.*

Sterling, Claire, "The Terrorist Network." The Atlantic, *Nov. 1978. $1.50.*

4
Energy: U.S. Dependence on Foreign Oil

- Should energy be a top U.S. foreign policy priority?
- How can we reduce oil imports?
- What strategies can best meet our energy future?
- Should we negotiate with OPEC to stabilize oil prices and supply?

ENERGY FACTS

▶ Oil provides 47% of U.S. energy, natural gas 27%, coal 18%, hydroelectric 4%, nuclear 4%.
▶ U.S. crude oil consumption in 1979 was 18.5 million barrels a day (MBD). (A barrel is 42 gallons.) Leading use (38%) is gasoline for motor transport.
▶ Net oil imports in 1979, 8.1 MBD; were 44% of U.S. oil consumption.
▶ U.S. consumes 30% of both world energy and oil.

BACKGROUND

By mid-20th century oil replaced coal as leading U.S. energy source. Through 1945 U.S. led world in oil exports, but in 1948 became net oil importer for first time. U.S. oil consumption rapidly outpaced domestic oil production, which peaked in 1970 at 9.6 MBD and has slowly declined since. Increasing oil imports have made up difference. Meanwhile, Europe and Japan in postwar boom switched from coal to oil—nearly all imported, mainly from Mideast.

Leading World Producers in 1979		**Leading Sources of U.S. Imports in 1979**	
	MBD		MBD
Soviet Union	11.3	Saudi Arabia	1.3
Saudi Arabia	9.0	Nigeria	1.1
U.S.	8.5	Libya	0.7
Iraq	3.0	Venezuela	0.7
Iran	2.6	Algeria	0.6
Nigeria	2.4	Canada	0.5
Kuwait	2.3	Mexico	0.4

Rise of OPEC. In 1959 major oil multinationals, which then controlled world oil trade, cut crude oil prices. This shock led Mideast oil exporters to join Venezuela in forming Organization of Petroleum Exporting Countries (OPEC). Not taken seriously at first, OPEC grew in power when Western dependence increased, oil market tightened in early 1970s.

Arab oil embargo against U.S. and Netherlands in Arab-Israeli war of Oct. 1973 revealed OPEC's new power. OPEC quadrupled crude oil prices to $11.65 per barrel in Jan. 1974, pushing Western economies into severe recession. Though oil crisis seemed to fade, U.S. oil imports 1973-79 increased 30%.

During Iran's 1978 revolution oil exports stopped for 69 days, then resumed at below half previous level. Led to world oil scramble. OPEC prices jumped from $12.70 per barrel to 1980 average $30 per barrel.

OIL PRODUCERS AND CONSUMERS

Massive dependence of U.S., Europe, Japan and most less-developed countries (LDCs) on OPEC oil gives oil exporters strong political weapon: they can threaten price hikes, oil boycotts against importing countries to gain leverage in disputes. Exporters, however, are also dependent: need Western markets, products and technology.

Rapid social change leading to revolution, as in Iran, could disrupt flow of oil. Conservative Gulf regimes may also produce less oil, keep more in ground, to prevent inflation from eating away oil earnings; they also fear that assets might be frozen by West in future crisis (see Issue No. 12). Finally, Soviet Union may become net oil importer in 1980s; could bring U.S.S.R. into dangerous competition for Gulf supplies.

Outside Mideast, Carter Administration has sought to improve ties with important new oil producers, Nigeria and Mexico. But oil linked with other issues. Mexico wants concessions on trade, illegal aliens. Nigeria, black Africa's biggest power, wants changes in U.S. policy toward southern Africa.

WORLD OIL PICTURE TODAY

U.S. oil dependence hurts world confidence in U.S. leadership. Oil import bill, about $2 billion in 1968, reached $40 billion in 1978, $60 billion in

1979. U.S. oil imports and dollar's weakness have been called 2 sides of the same coin.

Except for North Sea supplies, nearly all oil in Western Europe and Japan is imported. Allies sharply criticize U.S. energy policies; blame U.S. waste, massive imports for driving up world oil prices. Allies lean more toward Arabs than toward Israel on question of Palestinians.

Oil-poor LDCs hit hard by price increases; their combined payments deficit rose $11 billion to $36 billion total in 1979. Some have suffered drop in already low living standards.

U.S. ENERGY SUPPLY OUTLOOK

Imported oil. Current OPEC production of 30 MBD not expected to increase in 1980s; may decline.

Domestic oil production, level of proven reserves continue gradual decline. President Carter believes oil price decontrol will increase reserves and production; CIA estimates it will only slow decline.

Synthetic fuels ("synfuels"). U.S. has 2 trillion barrels of oil locked in shale formations in Western states, enough coal to last 300 years. But cost guesstimates on liquid fuel from these solids exceed $40 per barrel. Environmental, health and safety hazards abound. Even with government subsidies, synfuel projects will take years to develop.

Nuclear energy in deep trouble after 1979 accident at Three Mile Island. Investigating commission recommended fundamental changes in reactor construction, operation, regulation; even so, still might be "serious future nuclear accident." New nuclear reactor construction at a standstill.

Solar energy clean and inexhaustible. Solar units

for hot water, space-heating already cost-competitive in parts of the country; solar electricity generation 10-15 times more expensive than conventional sources, but costs dropping sharply. Advocates claim that with proper incentives, solar (including wind, waterpower and biomass conversion) could supply up to 25% of U.S. energy by year 2000. Other estimates lower.

<u>Conservation</u>. Some progress made under impact of rising oil prices: energy-saving industrial processes, better auto mileage, building insulation, etc. In 1974, a 1% rise in GNP required 1% more energy; now requires only 0.6% more. Harvard Business School, National Academy of Sciences reports urge conservation as least painful choice to meet energy needs. Others skeptical.

ENERGY PLANS—PRESIDENT, CONGRESS AND CANDIDATES

Watered-down version of April 1977 Carter energy plan, including gradual decontrol of natural gas prices, passed Congress Oct. 1978. In 1979 Carter began decontrol of domestic crude oil prices; in March 1980 Congress approved most of Carter "windfall profits" tax. Tax on decontrolled crude expected to raise $227 billion in next decade, with 60% going into general revenue; 15% energy and transportation programs; 25% energy aid to poor. Congress allocated $20 billion for synfuel development, also enacted standby gasoline rationing plan.

Presidential candidates call Carter measures insufficient. Rep. John B. Anderson (R-Ill.) proposes 50¢ per gallon gas tax (rebated through reduction in Social Security payroll tax) to cut consumption; Senator Kennedy (D-Mass.) and Governor Brown (D-Cal.) advocate gas rationing. Brown strongly for solar, strongly against nuclear power. All Republicans support nuclear power (as does Carter). Reagan opposes windfall profits tax, favors profit incentives to spur energy production.

ENERGY CHOICES: PRO AND CON

■ **Make reduction of oil imports a top priority.**
Pro: (1) Unless the U.S. achieves "energy independence," it will remain vulnerable to oil blackmail. (2) Unrestrained U.S. imports will boost world oil prices, add to inflation, hurt balance of payments, weaken dollar. (3) Inaction could provoke world scramble for energy supplies, even energy wars.
Con: (1) Cultivating good relations with oil producers is a better way to assure continued oil supply. (2) Reducing oil imports too fast means painful economic costs shared unequally by regions and economic groups. (3) At present oil remains less expensive, less damaging to environment than other energy sources.

■ **Meet U.S. energy needs more through conservation and solar energy; less through coal and nuclear power.**
Pro: (1) Conserving even a fraction of energy waste would yield large savings. (2) Solar energy and conservation have few health, environmental side effects. (3) Both inexhaustible; cannot be embargoed.

Con: (1) Drastic conservation means painful changes in ways Americans live, work, travel, consume. (2) Solar energy expensive, overrated, distant technology. (3) U.S. already has proven energy technologies—coal and nuclear.

■ **U.S., Europe and Japan should negotiate with OPEC to stabilize oil prices and supply.**
Pro: (1) There will be disruptions of supply and price in world oil market until OPEC and West reach general agreement. (2) OPEC has a stake in dialogue: members worried about inflation, health of investments in West. (3) Could bring new start in "North-South" relations.
Con: (1) OPEC would exact stiff terms for price stability. (2) Would introduce price rigidity in energy markets, disrupt world economy. (3) As oil demand slackens, normal market forces will lead to demise of OPEC.

Select Bibliography

"A Progress Report on Alternative Energy Sources." Fortune, *Sept. 24, 1979. $2.00.*

Parisi, Anthony J., "Creating the Energy-Efficient Society." The New York Times Magazine, *Sept. 23, 1979.*

Stobaugh, Robert and Yergin, Daniel, eds., Energy Future: Report of the Energy Project at the Harvard Business School. *New York, Random House, 1979. 353 pp. $12.95.*

5

Trade and the Dollar

- Is liberalized trade in the U.S. national interest?
- Does the U.S. need a stronger export promotion policy?
- Should the U.S. shore up the ailing dollar, even if it hurts?
- Are growing foreign investments in the U.S. a reason for concern?

FOREIGN TRADE FACTS

▶ In 1979 U.S. goods and services exported ($286.3 bil.) once again less than those imported ($286.6 bil.)—producing current-account deficit of $300 mil. But deficit less than in 1978 ($14 bil.) and 1977 ($14 bil.). Last surplus ($5 bil.) in 1976.

▶ 1 out of 8 U.S. industrial jobs, 1 out of every 5 U.S. farm dollars, depend on exports.

▶ Exports total 9% of U.S. GNP.

▶ Nearly 1/3 harvested acreage produces for export.

▶ U.S. imports 1/5 of raw materials essential to its economy, including following: bauxite, 99%; manganese ore, 98%; cobalt, 97%; tin, 86%; nickel, 70%; zinc, 58%; iron, 33%; and petroleum, 44%.

The Balance — Strong and Weak Spots		
($bil.)	1978	1979
Trade in Merchandise:	−34.2	−29.5
Oil	−40.4	−60.0
Manufactures	−4.8	+10.0
Agriculture	+14.5	+20.0
Other	−3.5	+0.5
Services and Transfers (Including Direct Investment)	+20.3	+29.2

Trade background. Since early 1900s U.S. shifted to lowering of tariffs as stimulus to world trade in what each country makes best (known as comparative advantage). Surge of protectionism after World War I culminated in Hawley-Smoot tariff of 1930, highest in U.S. history, which provoked retaliatory tariffs and near-collapse of world trade, contributing to 1930s Great Depression. Reciprocal Trade Agreements Act of 1934 began historic series of trade barrier reductions. From 1934 to 1979, average U.S. tariffs decreased from 47% to 8%; value of U.S. exports increased nearly 80-fold.

GATT. Post-World War II trade among industrialized countries encouraged by 1947 General Agreement on Tariffs and Trade (GATT). GATT provides negotiating framework for worldwide reduction of trade barriers. Sixth or Kennedy Round of GATT negotiations in 1967 eliminated many tariffs on industrial goods.

Tokyo Round. Seventh or Tokyo Round of GATT negotiations opened in 1973, finally completed in April 1979. Like Kennedy Round, will re-

U.S. Trade with Major Partners
(1979, $bil.)

	Exports	Imports	Trade Balance
Canada	36.4	38.9	−2.5
EEC	42.6	33.2	+9.4
Japan	17.6	26.3	−8.7
Non-OPEC LDCs	48.1	51.1	−3.0
OPEC	14.5	45.0	−30.5

duce industrial tariffs another 1/3, to a new low, average of 5-6%.

Most important accomplishment of Tokyo Round is attack on nontariff barriers to world trade. This agreement will (1) prohibit export subsidies; (2) streamline health and safety standards (which often act as disguised trade barriers); (3) establish uniform method of customs valuation; (4) open government procurement to foreign bidders; (5) cut red tape on import licenses; (6) establish need to demonstrate injury to domestic producers before governments can impose protectionist "safeguards" against imports.

Main thrust of Tokyo Round — freer trade and less government intervention to protect domestic producers — remains controversial. U.S. workers, especially in ailing steel, auto, textile and footwear industries, object that liberal trade rules, foreigners' dumping (selling goods below cost) threaten jobs.

THE DOLLAR

Dollar served as world's principal reserve currency held by central banks of trading nations throughout post-World War II era. U.S. balance-of-payments deficits (from capital outflows in private investments overseas, military expenditures, foreign aid) provided other nations with financial liquidity, which helped spur international trade and greatest quarter century of world economic growth in all history. Dollar, pegged to gold at $35 an ounce, truly was "good as gold."

But hemorrhage of dollars abroad, largely caused by expense of Vietnam war, led to global inflation and to President Nixon's decision in Aug. 1971 to end gold/dollar convertibility. Dollar devalued in Dec. 1971 and again in 1973. System of fixed exchange rates soon collapsed. Since then, world has limped along with slow growth in unsteady system of floating exchange rates.

Carter Administration at outset officially commited to let dollar fall or rise in market like any other commodity. But sharp drops in dollar's exchange value led to U.S. intervention in money markets in Nov. 1978 and again in Oct. 1979 to support dollar.

Dollar still world's most important currency, but beset with problems. Inflation in U.S., at 1980 rate of 18%, continues to run ahead of inflation in many other industrial countries. U.S. energy woes, including payments for OPEC oil at escalating prices (estimated bill for 1980 — $90 billion) contribute greatly to monetary instability, world inflation.

Fear also growing in U.S. that foreigners — especially OPEC countries — are using extra dollars to "buy up" America. Some critics believe that government should restrict foreign investment in U.S.

ALTERNATIVES TO PRESENT POLICY
■ **Restrict trade to protect U.S. industries, jobs.**

Pro: (1) Freer trade increases dependence on foreign producers. For national defense, self-sufficiency important. (2) U.S. must protect its own workers first. (3) Foreign governments will help their own producers regardless of trade agreement. U.S. must compete in same way. (4) Unequal trade concessions, as under Tokyo Round, will only cause further U.S. balance-of-payments problems.

Con: (1) Freer trade creates jobs for U.S. workers, opens new markets for U.S., especially in high technology and agriculture. (2) Faltering U.S. industries helped better by worker retraining, adopting new technology or product line. Protectionism only stopgap measure. (3) New trade barriers would harm ties with closest allies — Canada, Western Europe, Japan. (4) Freer trade increases competition, helps fight inflation.

■ **Establish a strong agency to promote exports.**

Pro: (1) Because of dollar devaluation, lower labor costs than trading partners, U.S. has great opportunity to increase exports. Government policy should aid this end. (2) Increased exports improve balance of payments, create jobs, foster growth. (3) Export promotion today hindered by conflicting policies of 7 Cabinet departments which restrict export sales for various reasons: human rights, national security, antitrust, antibribery, anti-Arab boycott, environment. Strong centralized agency necessary to streamline export promotion.

Con: **(1)** Business can determine profitability of exports itself; does not need more bureaucracy. **(2)** Trade promotion violates spirit of Tokyo Round, invites retaliation. May lead to harmful "trade war." **(3)** U.S. trade, because of great volume, has great potential political impact. Impossible to separate politics from foreign economic policy.

■ Take steps, even if painful, to strengthen dollar, renew U.S. monetary leadership.

Pro: **(1)** Imperative that inflation and energy dependency be brought under control — by drastic measures, if necessary. Success would greatly help dollar. **(2)** Our allies depend on U.S. dollar stability; instability hurts them and undercuts U.S. world leadership.

Con: **(1)** Financial discipline — in form of higher interest rates, higher energy prices, recession — imposes unfair burdens on poorer members of society. **(2)** It is no longer 1945. U.S. cannot be expected to bear burden of monetary leadership alone. Japanese yen and West German mark, or combination of currencies, must begin to assume reserve status also.

■ Restrict investment by foreigners in U.S.

Pro: **(1)** Foreign countries often hamper U.S. investors. We should follow suit. **(2)** Foreigners might gain control over sensitive technologies; might gain leverage in U.S. politics, undermine national security. **(3)** Foreign-controlled banks might — in an extreme case — divert funds in support of anti-U.S. or terrorist causes.

Con: **(1)** Action against foreign investment in U.S. will only provoke harmful retaliation. While foreign direct investment in U.S. totals $40 billion, U.S. direct investment abroad, $168 billion; latter makes net contribution to balance of payments of $12 billion annually. **(2)** Less than 1% of foreign direct investment in U.S. owned by OPEC countries. **(3)** Foreign companies in U.S. make net contribution to U.S. economy through increased competition, capital formation, jobs and service to U.S. consumer.

Select Bibliography

Cohen, Benjamin J., "Europe's Money, America's Problem." Foreign Policy, Summer 1979. $3.00.

"The Trade Debate." Department of State Publication 8942. USGPO, Washington, D.C. 20402, May 1978.

Zupnick, Elliot, "Foreign Investment in the U.S.: Costs and Benefits." HEADLINE Series 249. New York, Foreign Policy Association, April 1980. 80 pp. $2.00.

6

The UN and Third-World Development

- Does U.S. aid to UN development programs pay off?
- Can the U.S. get along with the "third world"?
- Can it get along without it?
- Should the poor nations get a larger share of the world's resources?

BACKGROUND

United Nations founded in 1945 in San Francisco. U.S., Latin America and Western Europe constituted majority of 51 charter members; only 5 Afro-Asian nations. As decolonization progressed, membership grew. In pivotal year 1960, 17 newly independent nations (16 African) admitted. 1980 UN membership: 152.

New majority are less-developed countries (LDCs) of "South" or third world. They outnumber developed countries (DCs) of "North" about 4 to 1. Third world can muster 2/3 vote to adopt resolutions in General Assembly (GA) and other bodies where 1-nation, 1-vote applies. Only in 15-member Security Council can permanent members (China, France, UK, U.S.S.R., U.S.) veto resolution supported by majority.

Third-World Profile

	Population (millions) mid '79	GDP Per Capita $ Amount 1978	Growth Rate % 1970-80	Literacy 1975 %	Life Expectancy 1977
Poorest countries	1,279	185	1.7	36	50
Middle-income countries	1,009	1,225	2.9	69	60
All developing countries	2,288	645	2.8	50	54

Source: World Bank

Nonaligned. Third-world coalition originated as political grouping of nonaligned states professing neutral stance on East-West issues. Founders: India's Nehru, Egypt's Nasser, Yugoslavia's Tito. First formal summit held in Belgrade, Yugoslavia, 1961; took anticolonial, anticold-war stand. Sixth summit (94 members) held in Havana, Cuba, 1979; elected Castro chairman. Pro-Moscow faction subsequently suffered setbacks. Majority of nonaligned denounced Soviet invasion of Afghanistan; thereupon Cuba's candidacy for Security Council seat failed for lack of votes.

Group of 77. Political grievances (southern Africa, Israel) aside, cement uniting third world is primarily economic. Following membership growth in 1960, GA proclaimed Decade of Development, set growth and aid targets for 1960s. In 1964, 77 LDCs (Group of 77, now numbering 120) formed UN Conference on Trade and Development, first of several development-related UN agencies.

New International Economic Order (NIEO). Third-world economic unity peaked in 1974. Oil producers' cartel proved LDCs could wield real power against DCs. In GA, LDCs proclaimed NIEO, right to larger share of world's resources.

U.S. rejected LDC demands in 1974; at 1975 special session agreed to help stabilize LDC export earnings, facilitate exchange of technology, etc. Session ended with unanimous resolution, but attempt at implementation in North-South conference (Paris, 1975-77) had meager results. North unsuccessfully pushed for energy cooperation. South unsuccessfully called for indexation (tying price of raw materials to export price of industrial goods); redeployment of industries to LDCs; moratorium on debts. Conference approved $1 billion aid fund for poorest and Common Fund to stabilize commodity export prices.

Brandt commission. International commission of eminent persons, chaired by former West German Chancellor Willy Brandt, warned in Feb. 1980 that unless there is "fundamental change" in North-South relations, world economy faces "somber future." Proposed tripling international development aid to annual rate of $50 billion-$60 billion in 5 years; universal taxation; more stable oil supplies, prices.

DEVELOPMENT TRENDS

Results of development drive to date very unequal (see table). Today there are 800 million "absolute poor" (compared with 600 million in 1970). By year 2000, even if LDC economic growth averages optimistic 5.6% a year, forecast is still 600 million very poor.

Population. Despite slowing growth rates, world population may not stabilize before reaching 10 billion in late 21st century. As demand increases, many renewable resources (cattle, fish, grain, trees, water) as well as nonrenewable minerals becoming scarcer. To reduce danger of famine, World Food Reserve and $1 billion International Fund for Agricultural Development created following 1974 World Food Conference.

Trade. Non-oil-exporting LDCs' trade hurt by recession in non-Communist DCs which buy 75% of LDC exports, and by rise in cost of oil, food imports. In 1974, oil cost LDCs 4% of export earnings; in 1980, 25%. LDCs forced to borrow heavily from international financial institutions, large private banks. In 1970s industrialized countries adopted *generalized system of preferences (GSP)* favoring LDC exports, but many exceptions and safeguards protecting DC industries weaken effect. *Tokyo Round* of multilateral trade negotiations calls for reductions in tariffs, but key LDC exports excluded; few LDCs signed. *Technology:* LDCs demand free transfer of "appropriate" technology, including high technologies. U.S. has stressed transfer of labor-intensive and "basic needs" technologies. Segments of U.S. organized labor, industry oppose technology transfer: claim it exports jobs.

Development assistance from 17 major industrialized nations, 1965-1978, fell from average

0.44% of GNP to 0.35%; U.S. down from 0.49% GNP to 0.27%, with 12 countries contributing higher percentage than U.S. Decrease due to recession; disillusionment with aid results; concern that aid has not trickled down to poorest. Larger share of remaining aid channeled through international financial institutions. In FY 1979 World Bank and affiliates made commitments totaling over $10 billion; 17 DCs gave $18 billion; OPEC gave $4.8 billion (est.).

CARTER ADMINISTRATION POLICY

At outset, Carter Administration sought to improve relations with *third world and nonaligned.* Speaking at Notre Dame University in 1977, Carter said, "We can no longer separate the traditional issues of war and peace from the new global questions of justice, equity and human rights. . . . We know that a peaceful world cannot long exist 1/3 rich and 2/3 hungry." President appointed Andrew Young U.S. Representative to UN; worked with black Africans to find solutions to Namibia, Rhodesia problems; made trip to Nigeria. Promised to double *foreign aid* in 5 years. Aid increased from $4.1 billion to $8.1 billion in inflated dollars; decreased as percentage of GNP. Initial FY 1981 request of $8.3 billion includes $2.96 billion security assistance (primarily for Israel, Egypt); $1.88 billion bilateral development aid; $1.9 billion for international financial institutions; $1.6 billion Food for Peace.

Before Soviet invasion of Afghanistan, Administration promoted development aid on humanitarian and economic grounds (LDCs fastest growing market—46% of all U.S. overseas sales in 1978; supplied 42% of U.S. imports). Since invasion, Administration stresses ideological competition, security. U.S. aid operations reorganized in 1979 for first time in 20 years under new International Development Cooperation Agency.

ALTERNATIVES TO PRESENT POLICY

■ **Reduce U.S. participation in UN, restrict contributions.**

Pro: (1) Third-world majority does not share U.S. values, goals. GA frequently platform for propaganda attacks on U.S. (2) U.S. contributions to UN and its agencies (even World Bank despite weighted voting) cannot be controlled by U.S.; some spent in unfriendly countries, on projects contrary to U.S. policy, e.g. in Vietnam. (3) Multilateral lending agencies have become too bureaucratized, centralized to do effective job.

Con: (1) U.S. efforts to improve relations with LDCs paying off. Example: Third world joined in UN vote denouncing Soviet aggression in Afghanistan, leaving Soviet bloc isolated. (2) UN and its agencies cannot legally accept restricted contributions. If U.S. insisted, it would paralyze, eventually destroy UN, other agencies. (3) UN and financial institutions have good record in promoting LDC growth; forum for North-South collaboration.

■ **Substantially increase development assistance.**

Pro: (1) U.S. needs LDC resources, markets more than ever for continued growth. Without exports to LDCs, 1974-75 recession would have been even deeper. **(2)** Dollars spent on development are returned many times over in form of increased trade, expanded investment opportunities. **(3)** Private investment, tied to short-term profits, is no substitute for government aid. **(4)** Development, not arms race, promotes lasting security.

Con: **(1)** Development assistance has not bought U.S. allies or friends. **(2)** No assurance aid will buy secure access to LDC resources, trade. **(3)** Private business investments in LDCs cost taxpayer nothing; are more responsive to market conditions. **(4)** Until inflation brought under control, no room for aid increase in Federal budget.

Select Bibliography

Great Decisions '78, '79 and 1980. *New York, Foreign Policy Association. $5.00. See chapters on International Development, Trade and the Dollar, The UN at 35.*

North-South: A Program for Survival. *Report of Brandt commission. Cambridge, Mass., MIT Press, 1980. 304pp. $4.95.*

"*U.S. Arms and Foreign Aid.*" Current History, *July-Aug. 1979. $2.00.*

7

Southern Africa

- What kind of political settlement should the U.S. strive for in Namibia?
- Should the U.S. give economic support to Zimbabwe?
- What policy toward South Africa will best protect U.S. interests?

FACTS

▶ Population. <u>South Africa</u>, 26 million, including 18.6 million blacks (70%), 2.4 million Coloreds of mixed ancestry (9%), 0.7 million Asians (2%), and 4.3 million whites (18%), of whom 3/5 are Afrikaner (Dutch ancestry), the rest of English ancestry.

<u>Zimbabwe</u> (formerly Rhodesia), 7.2 million, including 220,000 whites (3%). <u>Namibia</u>, 900,000—800,000 blacks, 100,000 whites.

▶ Per capita income. <u>South Africa</u>, whites $5,101; blacks $461. <u>Zimbabwe</u>, whites $8,800; blacks $816. <u>Namibia</u>, whites $5,525; blacks $325.

In 1978 U.S. replaced Britain as South Africa's leading trading partner. U.S. firms account for 20% of country's foreign direct investment.

U.S. Trade and Investment
(1978 $mil.)

	South Africa	Rhodesia*	Namibia
U.S. Exports	1,079	1	10
U.S. Imports	2,259	0.3	5
U.S. Direct Investment	1,994	110	12
Percentage of U.S. Direct Investment	1.2	0.07	—

*U.S. was complying with UN mandatory trade sanctions.

BACKGROUND

South Africa. Dutch settlers (Afrikaners) arrived at Cape of Good Hope in 1652, pushed back indigenous people, later fought Bantu tribes. British captured Cape Colony in Napoleonic wars; clashed with Afrikaners (Boers) over land, diamonds, gold throughout 19th century; prevailed in Boer War (1899–1902). British created self-governing Union of South Africa in 1910.

Whites joined to exclude blacks from political system. Afrikaner Nationalist party, in power since 1948, elaborated *apartheid* policy of white domination.

Apartheid policy brought before UN in 1952; South Africa called it internal affair. World condemned 1960 Sharpeville massacre of blacks; Security Council, with U.S. support, approved 1963 *voluntary* embargo on arms shipments to South Africa. During years of Nixon-Kissinger "tilt," U.S. protected South Africa with Security Council vetoes. South Africa suspended from UN General Assembly in 1974. Security Council in 1977 voted *mandatory* arms embargo after South African intervention in Angola 1975–76, repression of 1976 Soweto riots and suspicious death of black leader Steven Biko.

In 1979 Prime Minister P. W. Botha granted some union rights to black workers, opened review of tribal "homeland" policies that confine blacks, limit self-rule to poorest 13% of land. South African blacks consider changes cosmetic: basic demand, majority rule, still anathema to dominant whites.

Namibia, former German colony of South-West Africa, administered by South Africa under 1920 League of Nations mandate. South Africa in 1946 rejected UN trusteeship for Namibia; imposed apartheid. UN General Assembly in 1966 revoked South Africa's mandate; World Court in 1971 ruled its presence illegal.

Under pressure of world condemnation and expanding guerrilla war with SWAPO (South-West African People's Organization), South Africa in 1975 convened Turnhalle Conference, called for independent Namibia based on confederation of tribal states. UN majority condemned plan, viewed it as scheme to keep white control. In 1977 UN "contact group" of Western Security Council members (U.S., Britain, France, West Germany, Canada) began negotiations with SWAPO and South Africa. By Dec. 1979 it won their consent, in principle, to cease-fire plan, UN-supervised elections leading to Namibian independence. Many details unsettled.

Rhodesia (now Zimbabwe) settled by British colonists, named in 1890 for Cecil Rhodes. Britain's terms of independence for Rhodesia — black majority rule — rejected in 1965 by Prime Minister Ian Smith, who issued "unilateral declaration of independence" based on white minority rule. UN Security Council, with U.S. support, imposed limited economic sanctions on Rhodesia in 1966, total trade embargo in 1968. Sanctions hurt Rhodesia, despite covert evasion and open U.S. purchases (1971–77) of chrome.

Pressure on Rhodesia also military. Black nationalists in early 1960s formed rival groups, Zimbabwe African People's Union (ZAPU) headed by Joshua Nkomo, and Zimbabwe African National Union (ZANU) headed by Robert Mugabe. Banned in Rhodesia, both turned to guerrilla war, cooperated loosely in Patriotic Front.

Faced with protracted guerrilla war, Smith negotiated 1978 "internal settlement" with 3 black leaders, led by Bishop Abel Muzorewa. Agreement provided for qualified majority rule, with 10-year white veto over constitutional change. Muzorewa became president in June 1979. Patriotic Front, excluded from elections, rejected settlement; war continued.

Britain's Prime Minister Margaret Thatcher (elected May 1979) and Carter Administration resisted intense pressure to lift sanctions, recognize Muzorewa government. Under Commonwealth mandate, Britain got Muzorewa government and Patriotic Front agreement in London Dec. 1979 on new constitution, cease-fire and elections — major triumph. Constitution reserves 20 seats for whites, but no veto. Cease-fire supervised by Britain's Lord Christopher Soames. In Feb. 1980 elections, Mugabe won 57 of 100 seats, asked Nkomo, whites to join cabinet, urged reconciliation. Prince Charles presided at April 18 independence ceremonies.

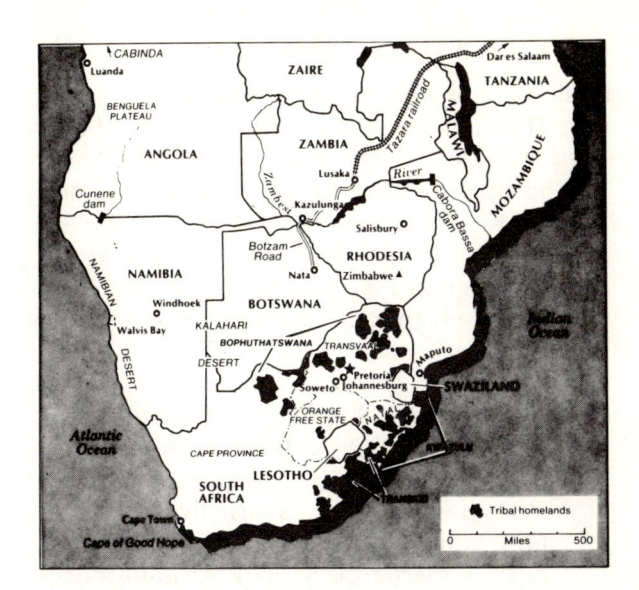

CARTER ADMINISTRATION POLICY

South Africa-U.S. relations chilly. U.S. 1977 call for 1-person, 1-vote absolutely rejected by Afrikaner leaders. U.S. endorsed Sullivan Code, called on U.S. firms in South Africa to enforce job equality. Apartheid, U.S. made clear, blocks improved relations. But U.S. seeks South Africa's help in peaceful resolution of Namibia's future.

Namibia. Still working through Western "contact group," U.S. hopes Zimbabwe peace will pave way for moderate Namibia solution.

Zimbabwe (Rhodesia). U.S. endorsed British efforts; lifted sanctions in Dec. 1979; recognized Zimbabwe. U.S. plans reconstruction-aid package for Zimbabwe and neighboring black states.

ALTERNATIVES TO PRESENT POLICY

■ Be wary of Mugabe and withhold aid.
Pro: (1) Mugabe remains avowed Marxist-Leninist. (2) Mugabe's forces stole election by intimidation. (3) Once power consolidated, he is likely to suppress opponents, expropriate whites, ally with Moscow. (4) Black African nations undemocratic, poor; not worth cultivating except Nigeria, which has oil, needs U.S. markets.

Con: (1) Mugabe played by rules; majority choice. U.S. support will strengthen his moderation. (2) Support for Mugabe best way to prevent Soviet presence. (3) World would condemn attempt now to install alternative to Mugabe. (4) Working with Mugabe will continue to improve important U.S.-black African strategic and trade ties.

■ Drop support of UN plan for Namibia.
Pro: (1) UN group would not monitor elections fairly. (2) UN plan would give power to Soviet-supported SWAPO. (3) South Africa will not ease apartheid with a Marxist state next door.

Con: (1) Would isolate U.S. (2) Would create pretext for Soviet and Cuban intervention. (3) Would not end low-level guerrilla war.

■ Curb economic ties with South Africa.
Pro: (1) Only tough steps — restricting export financing, discouraging investment, denying tax credits, loans, etc. — will convince South Africa that U.S. will not save apartheid. (2) Will increase U.S. influence with future black

leaders of South Africa. **(3)** Keeping diplomatic ties, U.S. can still talk with, influence white leaders.

Con: **(1)** Economic sanctions not enforceable; other countries will not join; will hurt U.S. business. **(2)** Will only raise black expectations, when in fact we cannot deliver. **(3)** Sanctions will not alter South Africa's policies.

■ Cooperate fully with South Africa.

Pro: **(1)** Only in context of cooperation, economic growth will South Africans contemplate racial change. **(2)** Like U.S., South Africa opposes Soviet thrust in Africa.

Con: **(1)** Periods of growth, substantial foreign investment historically periods of increased repression in South Africa. **(2)** Policy forces black nationalists into arms of U.S.S.R..

Select Bibliography

Deutsch, Richard, "High Stakes on Namibia." Africa Report, *Nov.-Dec. 1979. $2.25.*

"South Africa Under Botha." Foreign Policy, *Spring 1980. $3.00. Three points of view.*

Whitaker, Jennifer Seymour, "Conflict in Southern Africa." HEADLINE Series *240. New York, Foreign Policy Association, Aug. 1978. 96 pp. $2.00.*

8
China and Taiwan

- Has the U.S. moved too fast toward normalization?
- Is a "tilt" toward China in the U.S. long-term interest?
- Should the U.S. defend Taiwan if it is attacked?

BACKGROUND

Cold war. From 1949 (Communist victory in China and flight of defeated Nationalists to island province of Taiwan) to 1979, U.S. and People's Republic of China (PRC) had no diplomatic relations. PRC's early alliance with U.S.S.R. and intervention in Korean war (1950-53) deepened hostility; "world communism" seemed monolithic foe. In 1950 U.S. sent Seventh Fleet to patrol 100-mile-wide Taiwan Strait, prevent Communist liquidation of Nationalist government (Republic of China, or ROC). U.S. policy toward mainland China was based on nonrecognition, military containment, economic embargo. U.S. blocked PRC seat in UN. Recognized ROC as sole legal government; maintained close economic ties. Under 1954 mutual defense treaty U.S. committed to defend Taiwan.

1971: Thaw in U.S.-China relations begins as U.S. reappraises Asia policy following deterioration in Sino-Soviet relations in 1960s. PRC sees relationship with U.S. as counterweight to hostile Soviet Union. Nixon Administration sees thaw as increas-

---

Basic Facts

	China (PRC)	Taiwan (ROC)
Population	970 mil.	17 mil.
Growth rate	1.2%	2.1%
GNP	$407 bil.	$22 bil.
Per capita	$425	$1,295
Growth rate	4.5%	8.6%
Trade	$29 bil.	$34 bil.
With U.S.	$2.3 bil. (U.S. surplus $1.1 bil.)	$9.2 bil. (U.S. deficit $2.6 bil.)
Government leaders	Hua Guofeng, Chairman, Deng Xiaoping, Vice Premier	Chiang Ching-kuo, President

---

ing U.S. leverage against Soviet Union, spurring negotiated settlement in Vietnam, contributing to stable balance of power in Asia. In 1971, Nixon announces China visit; U.S. agrees to PRC UN seat but fails to save ROC's seat under dual-representation formula.

Nixon's Feb. 1972 trip to China ends with Shanghai communiqué, calling for progress toward normalization, trade, other contacts, diplomatic "liaison offices" in Washington and Peking. U.S. "does not challenge" Chinese view that Taiwan is part of

China, but retains option to defend Taiwan. Normalization stalls in 1975 as China insists U.S. derecognize Taiwan, remove remaining forces, terminate defense treaty. But death of Mao Zedong, Sept. 1976, and purge of radical "gang of four" open way for more pragmatic leadership eager for help in modernizing China.

Formal normalization announced Dec. 1978 by President Carter, Chairman Hua. U.S. recognizes Peking as sole legal government of China; ends diplomatic ties with Taiwan, effective Jan. 1, 1979; "acknowledges" Chinese position that Taiwan is part of China; will withdraw remaining troops from Taiwan and terminate mutual defense treaty Dec. 31, 1979. But whereas PRC maintains means of reuniting Taiwan with mainland is "entirely China's internal affair," U.S. expects Taiwan issue "will be settled peacefully."

Taiwan "outraged" by normalization and by U.S. failure to obtain Peking's guarantee not to use force against Taiwan. Taiwan Relations Act, with congressional warning to Peking that security of Taiwan is "of grave concern to the U.S.," signed April 1979. Established legal framework for unofficial relations with Taiwan. Embassy replaced by nongovernmental American Institute in Taiwan.

First year of normalization brings agreements on education exchanges; cooperation in science, technology; hydropower and water conservation; consular relations. Settlement in May 1979 of outstanding claims of U.S. citizens against PRC, and unfreezing of PRC assets in U.S., open door for full-scale shipping, air travel, banking relations. In July 1979, 3-year trade agreement signed. Gives

The People's Republic of China, home of one quarter of world's population.

PRC most-favored-nation (MFN) status, provides reciprocal trade concessions. China eligible for $2 billion in Export-Import Bank credits.

CARTER ADMINISTRATION POLICY

Normalization announcement touched off debate: (1) Was Congress adequately consulted? (Decision announced when Congress in recess.) (2) Were terms U.S. obtained best possible, and should it have accepted them? Critics argued U.S. betrayed old friend, should have insisted on binding assurances PRC would not use force against Taiwan. (3) Could President terminate treaty with Taiwan without congressional assent? Senator Goldwater (R-Ariz.) and 24 other legislators did not think so, filed suit against President. Federal court ruled for plaintiffs but Court of Appeals overturned decision and Supreme Court declined to review.

Administration, in reply to critics, said it had fully consulted members of Congress in course of year. Claimed it obtained important concessions—notably U.S. right, following 1-year moratorium, to resume selling Taiwan defensive military equipment. (In Jan. 1980 U.S. agreed to sell $280 million worth of antiaircraft, other defensive weapons.) Moreover, Carter, like Ford, stressed U.S. "interest in a peaceful resolution of the Taiwan issue."

U.S.-China-U.S.S.R. relations: "We will be cautious," Carter said in Jan. 1979, to avoid unbalanced relationship with Chinese and Russians. Evenhandedness also favored by Secretary of State Vance. But National Security Adviser Brzezinski favored closer relations with Peking. Some Pentagon experts wanted to modernize China's military equipment which, in many areas, is 15 years behind that of U.S., U.S.S.R. But Administration continued to forbid sale of weapons to PRC, though it did not oppose such sales by European allies.

Decision to submit July trade agreement with China to Congress in Oct. 1979 (approved in Jan. 1980) while continuing to withhold MFN status, credits from Soviet Union decisively tipped U.S. policy toward China. Tilted even further when Soviets invaded Afghanistan, Dec. 1979. In Jan. 1980 U.S. agreed to sell China a ground station for receiving information from Landsat Earth Resources Satellite. Station has possible military application. U.S. also now prepared to sell PRC "low" military technology but no weapons. Two countries agreed during Defense Secretary Brown's Jan. visit to China to "wider cooperation on security matters" in the future. Said Brown: if others threaten shared interests, U.S. and China can respond with "complementary action in the field of defense as well as diplomacy."

ALTERNATIVES TO PRESENT POLICY
■ **Exercise greater caution in normalization process.**
Pro: (1) China's revolution young and future course unpredictable. Today's leaders and their views may be repudiated tomorrow. (2) In no sense is China likely to share U.S. values or most U.S. interests in foreseeable future. Wise course is dispassionate, limited relationship.

Con: (1) China is major emerging power, will eventually be a superpower. U.S., by increasing bilateral relations, can encourage PRC to take more active, responsible role internationally. (2) China represents major potential market. Failure until 1980 to extend MFN and credits left U.S. in fourth place (after Japan, Hong Kong, West Germany) as trading partner.

■ **Resume evenhanded policy toward China, U.S.S.R.**
Pro: (1) Evenhanded policy critical to orderly expansion of relations with both countries, hence to world stability. (2) Tilt toward China liable to destabilize permanently U.S.-Soviet relations; provoke more hostile, aggressive Soviet policy; drag U.S. into China's quarrels and proxy wars with U.S.S.R. in Indochina and throughout developing world. (3) Strengthening China militarily would increase danger to Taiwan.

Con: (1) Major threat to peace is Soviet Union. U.S. should work with China, despite ideological differences, to balance and restrain U.S.S.R. (2) An evenhanded policy in name is not evenhanded in fact. Because Russians so far ahead of Chinese militarily and economically, evenhanded treatment in the past favored Russians, widened gap between U.S.S.R., China. **(3)** U.S. and China have parallel interest in resisting Soviet expansion—in Europe and Asia.

■ **Make unequivocal commitment to defend Taiwan in event of attack.**

Pro: **(1)** U.S. must defend Taiwan or lose credibility as ally. **(2)** U.S. economic interests (private investment and trade) in Taiwan far exceed those in China proper. **(3)** As PRC power grows, self-restraint on Taiwan will weaken.

Con: **(1)** Despite lack of written guarantees, PRC knows armed attack on Taiwan would risk rupturing vital relations with U.S. **(2)** No economic interests could justify risking war with world's most populous nation. **(3)** Formal guarantee would outrage China's view of its sovereign rights, disrupt U.S.-PRC relations for no gain.

Select Bibliography

"Chinese Vice Premiers Deng Xiaoping and Fang Yi Visit the United States." Department of State Bulletin, *March 1979.* $1.40.

Clough, Ralph N., "Taiwan's Future." The Wilson Quarterly, *Autumn 1979.* $4.00.

Harding, Harry, Jr., China and the U.S.: Normalization and Beyond. *New York, Foreign Policy Association, 1979. 32pp.* $1.50.

9

Cambodia, Vietnam and the Refugee Crisis

- Is the U.S. doing enough for Indochina's refugees?
- Can Cambodia be saved?
- If Thailand is attacked, should we go to its aid?
- Under what conditions should we normalize relations with Vietnam?

BACKGROUND

History. Modern Indochinese nations, Vietnam, Cambodia (later called Khmer Republic, now Kampuchea) and Laos, are products of millennia of migrations and conquest. Earliest migrants mostly from southern China. Most numerous people are Vietnamese. 1,000 years of Chinese rule over Vietnamese (until A.D. 939) left legacy of fear, resentment. Last Indochina conqueror was France (1884-1954). At 1954 Geneva conference, independent Vietnam divided provisionally into North (Communist) and South (backed by U.S.). North soon launched guerrilla attacks in South. U.S. sent combat forces to bolster South Vietnam, while North drew aid (no troops) from U.S.S.R., China.

U.S. involvement in Indochina peaked in 1968, when U.S. had 549,500 troops in South Vietnam. North's surprise "Tet offensive" early in 1968 undermined U.S. public support for war, ended troop reinforcement. Nixon Administration started "Vietnamization," reducing U.S. forces even while extending war to Laos, Cambodia. U.S. and North Vietnam signed complex Paris peace agreement in 1973, never implemented. Early in 1975 South Vietnamese army collapsed; Saigon fell in April. Cambodia's capital, Phnom Penh, fell to Communist Khmer Rouge shortly before Saigon fell. Lao Communists consolidated control over Laos few months later.

In postwar Vietnam, population 51 million, government moved unemployed, surplus urban labor in South to "new economic zones"; placed up to 200,000 political prisoners in "reeducation centers." Nationalized private trade in 1978, drove out Vietnamese of Chinese ancestry (ethnic Chinese) who fled by boat. In Kampuchea, brutal leader Pol Pot evacuated cities, towns at gunpoint; massive death toll. In Laos, mountain people, who helped U.S., fled on foot to Thailand.

Kampuchea attacks Vietnam; Vietnam invades Kampuchea; China invades Vietnam. Traditional Vietnamese-Cambodian hostility erupted soon after Communist victories: Kampuchea attacked islands claimed by both countries. Vietnam moved toward Soviet alliance; in Nov. 1978 signed 25-year friendship treaty. In Dec. 1978 Vietnam invaded Cambodia; overthrew Pol Pot, who continues guerrilla war with 30,000 troops. Vietnam installed Heng Samrin government in Phnom Penh; supported by

200,000 Vietnamese troops. China retaliated by invading northern Vietnam, Feb. 1979; both sides claimed victory in 17-day war. With Vietnam showing no signs of pulling out, some analysts believe its objective is destruction of Kampuchea, expansion into Thailand. Others see Vietnamese role as defensive: flanked by hostile allies, China and Kampuchea, struck weaker.

The three states of Indochina—Vietnam, Laos and Cambodia (now known as Kampuchea)—were part of the French overseas empire until 1954. The 'sick man' of Southeast Asia, the area is buffeted by war, famine and oppression.

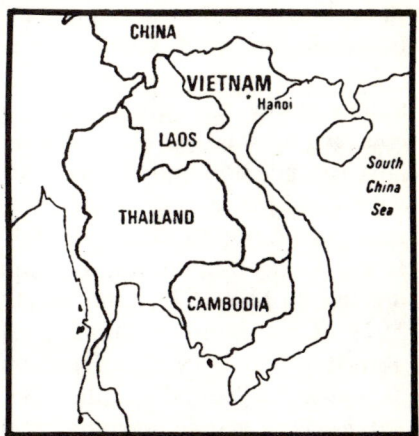

<u>Kampuchea</u>, once region's granary, now barely kept alive by international relief. Bombing, Pol Pot holocaust, invasion, continued guerrilla war have reduced Khmer population from 7 million – 8 million in 1970 to estimated 4 million. Malnutrition, disease widespread; pockets of starvation. Much of seed stocks eaten or destroyed in 1979.

<u>International relief</u> effort mounted by International Red Cross, UN Children's Fund, private organizations, but food, medical supplies, doctors blocked by government for months from entering country. U.S. called on Hanoi, Moscow to open

routes. Most supplies that got through remained in warehouses until Feb. 1980. Some suspect deliberate Vietnamese policy of genocide; others blame lack of transportation, government's fear food would aid insurgents.

Another grave food crisis emerged spring 1980. 150,000 sick, hungry refugees in camps in Thailand, which opened border in Nov. 1979 after being severely criticized for forcing 45,000 Khmers back into their country; 600,000 more near border.

Indochina's other refugees. Since 1975, more than 1 million Lao, Khmers and Vietnamese (not counting most recent flood of Khmers, who do not have refugee status and can be forcibly repatriated) have sought asylum in neighboring countries. Refugee population in Thailand, Malaysia, Indonesia, Hong Kong, Singapore, Philippines peaked at 380,000 in May 1979; down to 290,000 by end of 1979. Under international pressure, Vietnam agreed in July 1979 to halt boat-refugee traffic for "a reasonable period of time." By Jan. 1980 Vietnamese boat people down to 2,000 a month (from 60,000 a month mid-'79), but increasing number fleeing in dangerous treks across Kampuchea.

Refugees permanently resettled include 300,000 in U.S.; 170,000 in other non-Communist countries (60,000 in France, 35,000 in Canada, 35,000 in Australia); 250,000 Vietnamese resettled in China.

CARTER ADMINISTRATION POLICY

Vietnam. U.S. has no diplomatic relations with Vietnam; maintains embargo on trade, investment; 87 U.S. servicemen still on missing-in-action (MIA) list. U.S.-Vietnamese normalization talks broke down in 1977: U.S. rejected Vietnam's insistence on reconstruction aid as precondition. Congress in 1977 prohibited "reparations, aid, or any other form of payments" to Vietnam. In fall 1978 Vietnam dropped aid condition, but now U.S. rules out normalization for time being as result of Vietnam's invasion of Kampuchea, close ties with U.S.S.R., expulsion of ethnic Chinese.

Strategic interests. U.S. seeks to maintain current equilibrium in Asia and Pacific, not allow any single power to achieve preponderance. Vietnam and growth of Soviet power seen as main destabilizing threats; China, for moment at least, as counterbalance. U.S. "committed to keeping a strong, flexible military presence in the region" (Vance). Security commitment to Thailand, embodied in 1954 Southeast Asian defense pact, remains in force.

Kampuchea. Vance called Khmers "a people on the verge of extinction." U.S. deplored brutal violations of human rights under Pol Pot, but, along with most governments, continues to recognize Chinese-backed Khmer Rouge, not Heng Samrin. In 1979 U.S. approached Vietnam, U.S.S.R., China, others in search of political settlement based on withdrawal of Vietnamese troops, creation of independent Khmer government, end to external interference. (Senator Kennedy, Rep. Stephen J. Solarz [D-N.Y.] favor international conference of superpowers, China, Southeast Asian nations leading to withdrawal of Vietnamese from Kampuchea, independence, noninterference by others.)

<u>Kampuchea relief</u>. Critics claim Administration slow to respond to famine. In Nov. 1979 President

signed $60 million additional aid authorization for refugees in Kampuchea, $9 million for Khmers in Thailand. Total U.S. commitment in FY 1980: $105 million.

Indochina refugees. In FY 1980 U.S. admitted 168,000 refugees under special "parole" program authorized by Attorney General. Doubled admission rate in mid-1979 from 7,000 to 14,000 a month. Priority given to refugees with close relatives in U.S., former government employees. 1980 Refugee Act raises ceiling on annual refugee admissions to 50,000; empowers President to admit more after consulting Congress.

ALTERNATIVES TO PRESENT POLICY

■ **Assure Kampuchea's survival by convening conference of all governments concerned to neutralize country.**

Pro: (1) Economic and political survival of Kampuchea are inseparable. (2) Only international action can stop destruction of Kampuchea and its people in murderous war between Khmer Rouge, aided by China, and Heng Samrin forces, aided by Vietnam and Soviet allies. (3) Only neutralization, as part of regional settlement endorsed by all governments concerned, can avert tragedy.

Con: (1) China, Soviet Union, Vietnam, whose agreement would be essential, have shown no support for neutralization or convening an international conference. (2) U.S. lacks influence in region to turn situation around. (3) The most U.S. can do is to continue supporting Kampuchea refugees in Thailand and rely on Heng Samrin regime to distribute relief inside Kampuchea.

■ **Normalize relations with Vietnam.**

Pro: (1) By normalizing relations, as we eventually did with China, U.S. would not be endorsing Vietnamese policies but would gain regular channel through which to pursue MIA, human rights, refugee issues as well as listening post the better to influence Hanoi's policies. (2) Would help Vietnam diversify its foreign relations, reduce dependence on U.S.S.R. (3) Hanoi government is a durable fact and sooner we have contact with it the better.

Con: (1) To normalize relations with this regime against which thousands of Americans fought and died is unthinkable. (2) Whatever we may say, normalization would be seen as condoning aggression in Kampuchea, human rights violations, expulsion of boat people. (3) Would *not* be likely to weaken Soviet-Vietnamese ties.

Select Bibliography

"Humanity" and "Vietnam." Great Decisions 1980. *New York, Foreign Policy Association, 1980. $5.00.*

Shawcross, William, "The End of Cambodia?" The New York Review of Books, *Jan. 24, 1980. $1.00.*

"U.S. Program to Assist the World's Refugees." Department of State Bulletin, *Oct. 1979. $1.40.*

10

The Caribbean and Central America

- Should the U.S. uphold human rights in Central America even when the violating governments are traditional U.S. allies?
- Should we normalize relations with Cuba?
- Should we increase economic assistance in the region?

FACTS

▶ Population: Of 11 Caribbean nations, largest are Cuba (9.6 mil.), Dominican Republic (5 mil.), Haiti (4.7 mil.), Jamaica (2.1 mil.). Puerto Rico (3.4 mil.) is U.S. commonwealth. St. Lucia (120,000) largest of tiny eastern Caribbean republics. Of 6 Central American states, Guatemala largest (6.6 mil.), Panama smallest (1.8 mil.). Population growth rate in Central America, 2.9%; Caribbean, 2.0%.

▶ Per capita income in Caribbean ranges from $2,910 in Trinidad and Tobago to $260 in Haiti. In Central America, range is from $1,540 in Costa Rica to $480 in Honduras.

▶ New nations in Caribbean include St. Vincent (1979), St. Lucia (1979), Dominica (1978), Grenada

(1974), Bahamas (1973). Central American republics, except Panama (1903), independent since 1830s.

▶ Investment and trade. Caribbean and Central America account for less than 3% of U.S. trade and U.S. direct foreign investment; 8% of U.S. world trade shipped through Panama Canal.

By contrast, Caribbean and Central American economies (except Cuba's) depend heavily on U.S. ties. U.S. tourism important for Caribbean islands. U.S. main customer for coffee, chief export of Costa Rica, El Salvador, Guatemala, Haiti, Honduras and Nicaragua; sugar (Dominican Republic); alumina and bauxite (Jamaica). Since 1974 commodity prices have not kept up with world inflation, causing hardship. One result: increased emigration and illegal entry into U.S.

HISTORICAL BACKGROUND

U.S. defeated Spain in 1898 war, occupied Cuba, annexed Puerto Rico and began deep involvement in affairs of Caribbean basin. In 1903 President Theodore Roosevelt encouraged a revolution in Panama, secured U.S. rights to build Canal. 1904 Roosevelt Corollary to Monroe Doctrine justified U.S. intervention in Caribbean, seen as necessary to bar European encroachment and, after 1914, to defend Panama Canal—vital to commerce and U.S. 2-ocean Navy.

Franklin D. Roosevelt's 1933 Good Neighbor policy forswore U.S. intervention. But promise did not survive cold war. U.S. used CIA to overthrow elected leftist President Jácobo Arbenz in Guatemala in 1954; attempted to overthrow Fidel Castro in Cuba but failed in 1961 Bay of Pigs disaster. U.S. broke diplomatic ties with Cuba in 1961, cut off trade in 1962; neither yet restored. In Oct. 1962 showdown, Moscow withdrew nuclear missiles from Cuba, but close Moscow-Havana alliance remains.

In 1965 President Johnson sent Marines to Dominican Republic to prevent "another Cuba." But U.S. interest in region waned once seen that revolution not exported so easily. Nixon and Ford Administrations began to thaw relations with Cuba.

CARTER ADMINISTRATION POLICY

Human rights major emphasis in President Carter's inaugural address. Administration manipulated military, economic aid to pressure regional rights violators, including Nicaraguan dictator and longtime U.S. friend, Anastasio Somoza Debayle.

Nicaragua. After Sandinista rebellion against Somoza broke out in 1978, U.S. policy erratic. U.S. would not defend repressive Somoza regime, but also attempted to prevent Sandinistas, with strong Marxist elements, from coming to power. This failed. Somoza fled Nicaragua July 1979; Sandinista-led coalition took over. Despite mutual suspicion, U.S. and new government worked together fairly well. Sandinistas kept role for private enterprise, adopted nonaligned stance; said they do not want "another Cuba," but, after Somoza, "another Nicaragua." U.S. gave Nicaragua $8 million in emergency aid; Congress considering additional $75 million.

Much instability also in Guatemala and El Salvador; U.S. hoped to shape moderate political course. In Feb. 1980 American pressure prevented right-wing coup in El Salvador. But extremist political violence there unabated: human rights advocate Archbishop Oscar Arnulfo Romero assassinated in March.

Panama Canal treaties, concluded under Carter after 13 years of negotiations, will give Panama control over Canal in stages ending Dec. 31, 1999; guarantee Canal's neutrality and U.S. ships' access thereafter. Treaties approved April 1978, despite intense opposition. Critics charged U.S. "strategic retreat"; Administration answered that Canal of little strategic value in postcolonial nuclear age.

Cuba. In Jan. 1977 Carter Administration renewed steps to improve relations with estranged Cuba. U.S. travel ban lifted; Cuba, in turn, released over 450 Americans, 3,600 Cuban political prisoners. Two sides agreed on maritime and fishery boundaries; established diplomatic "interest sections" in Havana and Washington; held talks on drug traffic and terrorism.

Normalization stalled, however, when Cuba sent 16,000 troops to Ethiopia in 1977 and refused to withdraw over 20,000 from Angola, present since 1975. Administration refuses to improve relations further until Cuban troops exit Africa. Remaining bilateral issues include Guantánamo naval base; $1.8 billion in U.S. expropriation claims against Cuba. U.S. also concerned by Castro's pro-Soviet leadership of nonaligned movement; Soviet "combat brigade" in Cuba; Cuba's regional influence.

Other Caribbean nations. The Dominican Republic showed signs of healthy democracy with

From *Encyclopedia of Latin America* by Helen Delpar. Copyright © 1974 by McGraw-Hill, Inc. Used with the permission of the McGraw-Hill Book Company.

peaceful 1978 election of President Silvestre Antonio Guzmán Fernández.

In Haiti, repression by government of Jean-Claude Duvalier continued, as did economic stagnation; 10,000 Haitians in south Florida illegally, seeking jobs unavailable in Haiti. Jamaica, with bauxite earnings down, oil import bills up, recorded 5th straight GNP decline since 1974.

Puerto Rico will hold 1981 plebiscite on its political future. Commonwealth status, dating from 1952, has had majority backing because of economic advantages. U.S. statehood gaining in popularity; independence supporters remain few.

New island ministates of eastern Caribbean troubled by economic hardship, political upheaval. Self-proclaimed "radical leftist," Maurice Bishop, led coup in Grenada, March 1979. He later received Cuban medical, agricultural, military aid—worrisome to Washington. In June 1979 another corrupt regime fell in Dominica; political unrest also in St. Lucia and St. Vincent.

Carter Administration's attention to Caribbean stems in part from interest in "containing Cuba." But it has stressed economic progress, regional cooperation in this area, referred to as "America's 3rd border." 1980 U.S. aid to Caribbean will total $155 million—5 times 1975 figure, highest per capita U.S. assistance in developing world.

ALTERNATIVES TO PRESENT POLICY

■ **Back all pro-U.S. governments in the region, regardless of human rights record.**

Pro: **(1)** Top priority must be to support friends, keep out Soviet, Cuban influence. **(2)** If U.S. is patient, dictators will make internal reforms as matter of self-preservation. **(3)** Only pro-American regimes protect U.S. investment, which benefits us and brings economic progress to entire region. **(4)** Respect for human rights cannot be imposed; meddling destabilizing.

Con: **(1)** Top priority should be to uphold region's democratic tradition. **(2)** U.S. backing for repressive governments unwise. Immense costs in human suffering, damage to U.S. prestige; will only spark radicalism and violence. **(3)** Private investors deal successfully with governments of many ideologies. **(4)** Under Carter pressure, human rights record in region has improved.

■ **Resume trade, normalize relations with Cuba.**

Pro: **(1)** U.S. cannot exert much influence on Cuban behavior unless it establishes relations. **(2)** Diplomatic isolation and trade embargo only increase Cuba's ties to Soviet Union. **(3)** Trade embargo only hurts U.S. business.

Con: **(1)** Normalizing relations now would mean that we accept Cuban meddling in Africa. **(2)** Trade embargo makes Cuba dependent on Soviet subsidies—costly burden for Soviets at no expense to ourselves. **(3)** U.S. unlikely to get much business in socialist Cuba.

■ **Give priority to economic development, regardless of politics or human rights.**

Pro: **(1)** Firm economic basis necessary for political stability, respect for human rights. **(2)** Constructive U.S. presence needed to outweigh Cuba's influence. **(3)** Jobs in Caribbean needed to stem tide of immigrants to U.S.

Con: **(1)** Not financial aid but guaranteed commodity prices, more access to U.S. market main economic demands of region. Costly to U.S. economic interests. **(2)** Right-wing governments use aid to enrich the rich. **(3)** Left-wing governments cannot be bought with aid.

Select Bibliography

Atlas World Press Review. *"What Next in Central America?"* Dec. 1979, and *"Nicaragua: Triumph of Moderation?"* Jan. 1980. $1.50 each.

Riding, Alan, *"Nicaragua: A Delicate Balance."* The New York Times Magazine, *Dec. 2, 1979.*

"U.S. Relations with the Caribbean and Central America." Current Policy *No. 117, Dec. 1979. Bureau of Public Affairs, Department of State, Washington, D.C. 20520.*

11

The Arab-Israeli Conflict

- Should the U.S. press Israel to make new concessions on Palestinian rights?
- Should the U.S. deal with the PLO?
- Should the U.S. withhold advanced weapons from Egypt?
- Should the U.S. disengage and let Egypt and Israel seek peace at their own pace?

BACKGROUND

U.S. interests in Mideast important — and conflicting. U.S. morally and politically committed to survival of Israel — within borders still in dispute. But also needs good relations with Israel's adversaries: Arab (and Iranian) oil vital to Western economies; stable governments in region a bulwark against chaos and anti-U.S. hostility, whether inspired locally or by Soviets. But Arab grievance against Israel generates hostility toward U.S.

U.S. has sought to reconcile conflicting interests through peace settlement between Israel and all its neighbors. Egyptian-Israeli peace treaty of 1979 viewed as major step, but issue of Palestinian rights still blocks general settlement.

ISRAEL and Occupied Territory

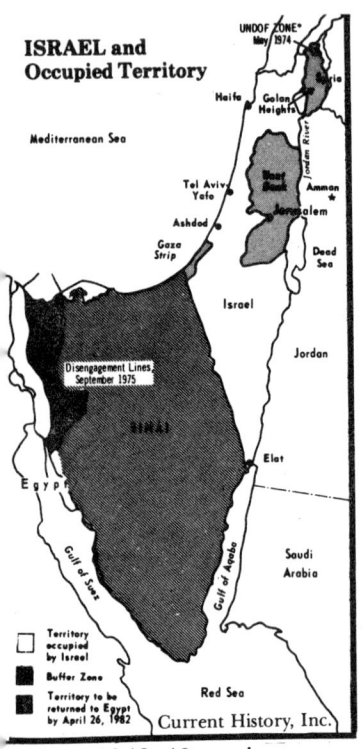

Map labels: UNDOF ZONE* May 1974; Haifa; Golan Heights; Mediterranean Sea; Tel Aviv Yafo; Ashdod; Gaza Strip; Jerusalem; Amman; Jordan River; Dead Sea; Israel; Jordan; Disengagement Lines, September 1975; SINAI; Egypt; Elat; Gulf of Suez; Gulf of Aqaba; Saudi Arabia; Red Sea; Territory occupied by Israel; Buffer Zone; Territory to be returned to Egypt by April 26, 1982; Current History, Inc.

Historical background.

Ancient land of Palestine, after 4 centuries of rule by Ottoman Turks, ruled by Britain from 1923 to 1948 under League of Nations mandate. These years saw influx of Zionists seeking promised "Jewish national home" and, from 1933, fleeing Nazi persecution. Jews clashed with resident Arabs. In 1947 the UN voted to partition Palestine into an Arab and a Jewish state. Arab states rejected partition, Britain withdrew; Arabs fought unsuccessful war in 1948–49 against new state of Israel. More than 500,000 Jews fled Arab countries, settled in Israel; similar number of Arabs fled Palestine, became refugees mainly in neighboring Arab states where umbrella organization of resistance, Palestine Liberation Organization (PLO), originated in 1964. Palestinians' future, unresolved by Arab-Israeli wars in 1956, 1967 and 1973, still at heart of conflict.

In Six-Day War of June 1967, victorious Israel seized territory from Egypt, Jordan and Syria over 3 times its pre-1967 size (see map). UN Security Council in Nov. 1967 adopted Resolution 242, containing peace guidelines: calls for Israel to withdraw "from territories" occupied in 1967 war and for all parties to respect each other's "right to live in peace within secure and recognized boundaries."

Ambiguity surrounds words "from territories." Arabs say they mean "*all* territories." Israel maintains withdrawal to pre-1967 borders would contradict provision in 242 for "secure" boundaries: villages inside Israel vulnerable to shelling from Golan Heights. Also, pre-1967 Israel at narrowest point only 12 miles wide. Menahem Begin government which took office in 1977 adds outright claim of sovereignty over West Bank of Jordan as biblical land of Judea and Samaria, promised by God to Jewish people.

In Oct. 1973 war Soviet-armed Egypt and Syria achieved surprising success before Israel, resupplied with airlifted U.S. arms, defeated both. The war brought U.S. and Soviet Union to brink of superpower confrontation, while Arab oil producers briefly embargoed shipments to the U.S. Then Secretary of State Kissinger's "shuttle diplomacy" (1974–75) achieved troop disengagements in the Sinai and Golan Heights. But no progress made on Palestinian issue.

PLO, backed by Arab oil money, strengthened since Oct. war. Arab summit in Rabat, Morocco, Oct. 1974, recognized it as "sole legitimate representative of the Palestinian people." Weeks later PLO chief Yasir Arafat addressed UN General Assembly, which gave PLO observer status.

PLO guerrilla raids into Israel from Lebanon brought heavy Israeli reprisals. Syria in 1976, then UN in 1978 sent troops to keep fighting in Lebanon from erupting into new war with Israel. PLO, only visible political champion of Palestinian cause, has never abandoned official aim to replace Israel with secular Palestinian state. Israel and U.S. view it as "terrorist," refuse to deal with it.

CARTER ADMINISTRATION POLICY

Geneva, then Jerusalem. In 1977 the new Carter Administration first sought comprehensive peace through a reconvened Geneva conference (deadlocked and adjourned since Dec. 1973), but frustrated by question of Palestinian representation.

In Nov. 1977 "Geneva strategy" was bypassed by Egyptian President Sadat's dramatic trip to Jerusalem. Way was open to tackle 2 tough issues: bilateral peace between Egypt and Israel and — linked to this by Egypt — solution of Palestinian question. Sadat-Begin negotiations, plus personal intervention of President Carter, achieved breakthrough at Camp David, Sept. 1978. Egyptian-Israeli peace treaty signed March 1979. First step, all 3 hoped, toward overall Arab-Israeli peace.

Treaty terms. Each side won major concessions. Israel got peace with its most populous and militarily powerful neighbor. Relations fully normalized, ambassadors exchanged Feb. 1980 upon completion of Israel's withdrawal from 2/3 Sinai. Egypt pledged to sell Israel 40,000 barrels of oil per day from Sinai fields. U.S. agreed to new 3-year $3.8 billion aid package for Israel, guaranteed its oil supply for 15 years, reiterated pledges to Israel's security. Egypt won return of Sinai, to be completed by April 1982, and $1.8 billion in U.S. assistance.

Palestine linkage. As part of peace treaty, Israel had to agree to "autonomy," to be defined by May 1980, for Palestinian Arabs in occupied territories. Sadat wants "autonomy" to approach Palestinian sovereignty; Begin wants it narrowly defined. In early 1980 2 sides remained far apart on security, land, water, Jewish settlements and Jerusalem.

17 Arab League states, including Saudi Arabia and Jordan, severed diplomatic ties with Egypt in March 1979, continue to attack Egypt's separate peace. Sadat calls Egypt "island of stability" in Arab world, and U.S., after Soviet invasion of Afghanistan, began 5-year program to arm Egypt with $4 billion of modern weapons, including F-16 fighters. Israel not happy with U.S. plans to arm Egypt. But March 1979 treaty itself — apart from autonomy negotiations — unfolding with remarkable ease.

U.S.-Israeli tensions persisted after signing of peace treaty. Carter Administration criticized Israel's bombing strikes in southern Lebanon; Israel's West Bank settlement policies; and Israel's Nov. 1979 arrest and threatened deportation (later rescinded) of Nablus mayor Bassam Shaka.

Israel, in turn, upset by Andrew Young's secret meeting with PLO's UN observer (revelation of which led in Aug. 1979 to Young's resignation), and U.S. black leaders' "dialogue" with PLO.

Two nations sparred again March 1980 when U.S. voted for unanimous UN Security Council resolution to rebuke Israel for settlements in occupied territories. Carter quickly disavowed vote, but policy confusion infuriated Arabs, Israel and many American voters.

ALTERNATIVES TO PRESENT POLICY

■ **Pressure Israel to make new concessions on Palestinian rights.**

Pro: (1) U.S. has its own interests in Mideast; should not let Israel dictate policy. (2) Israel's security depends less on *location* of borders than on ending neighbors' hostility; real Palestinian autonomy is unavoidable price. (3) If Israel not flexible, it may spell disaster for Sadat and Arab moderates. (4) Israel should negotiate *now*, from position of military strength.

Con: (1) U.S. pressure might lead Israel to abandon autonomy negotiations. (2) Unwelcome U.S. initiative would lead Israel to mobilize its friends in U.S., paralyze U.S. policy. (3) Pressuring Israel discourages Arab moderation, rewards Arab intransigence. (4) U.S. abandonment of its friend Israel ominous signal to U.S. allies worldwide.

■ **Deal directly with PLO.**

Pro: (1) U.S. acknowledgement of Palestinians' representatives long overdue. (2) Would improve U.S. standing in Arab world. (3) Some PLO factions believed to favor peace with Israel in exchange for Palestinian state. U.S. influence could strengthen moderates.

Con: (1) U.S. should not recognize or negotiate with the PLO so long as it does not recognize Israel's right to exist. (2) Move would signal U.S. approval of terrorism. (3) PLO has never wavered from objective of destroying Israel.

■ **Provide no new weapons to Egypt.**
Pro: (1) We may repeat same mistake we made in selling arms to the shah of Iran. (2) Who knows who will follow after Sadat? New weapons may be used someday against Israel.
Con: (1) Egypt needs to replace obsolete Soviet arms for defense. (2) Aiding Sadat strengthens peacemakers; bolsters U.S. position in region.

■ **Disengage, let Egypt and Israel seek peace at their own pace.**
Pro: (1) Foolish for U.S. to risk prestige at each step in negotiations. (2) Arabs dare not attack Israel; Israel can never have peace until it accepts some Palestinian entity. Both must discover these facts for themselves.
Con: (1) Instability growing. Without active U.S. mediation, war may break out again. Arabs will then turn oil money into weapons, use them against Israel again. (2) If U.S. ignores Arab political goals, Saudi Arabia and Jordan may swing against us, look to Soviets for help.

Select Bibliography

Ajami, Fouad, "The Struggle for Egypt's Soul." Foreign Policy No. 35, Summer 1979. $3.00.

Feith, Douglas J., "The Settlements and Peace." Policy Review No. 8, Spring 1979. Published by the Heritage Foundation, 513 C St., N.E., Washington, D.C. 20002. $3.00.

Heller, Mark, "Begin's False Autonomy." Foreign Policy No. 37, Winter 1979–80. $3.00.

12

Iran, Afghanistan and the Persian Gulf

- ✔ Is the Persian Gulf of vital interest to the U.S.?
- ✔ Do we need a Rapid Deployment Force in the Persian Gulf region?
- ✔ Should the U.S. seek to revive the "Nixon Doctrine"?
- ✔ What should—or can—the U.S. do about Afghanistan?

Persian Gulf States in 1980

	Population (millions)	Oil Production (mil. barrels per day)	Armed Forces
Iran	39.3	2.6	415,000
Iraq	12.7	3.0	222,000
Saudi Arabia	8.0	9.5	44,500
Kuwait	1.2	2.3	11,100
Oman	0.9	0.3	19,200
United Arab Emirates	0.9	1.8	25,000

Important Neighbors

	Population (millions)	Oil Production (mil. barrels per day)	Armed Forces
Afghanistan	21.4	—	ca. 35,000 (+75,000 Soviets)
Pakistan	80.2	0.01	429,000
Egypt	40.5	0.5	395,000
Israel	3.8	—	166,000

Persian Gulf oil as percentage of total oil consumption: Japan 73%; France 71%; Italy 61%; West Germany 43%; UK 25%; U.S. 13%; Canada 7%.

BACKGROUND

History. U.S. companies began to obtain oil concessions in Persian Gulf in 1920s; in Saudi Arabia in 1933. British influence in Gulf, paramount since 19th century, declined after World War II, when U.S. assumed Britain's security role. Under "Nixon Doctrine" U.S. sold sophisticated military weaponry to oil-rich Iran and Saudi Arabia, relied on those "twin pillars" to keep oil flowing, keep out Soviet and radical influence, minimize U.S. military commitments in region. 1970s also saw power shift from oil multinationals to Organization of Petroleum Exporting Countries, cartel of oil-producing governments, most of whose key members are in Gulf.

Gulf peoples Muslims of Sunni and Shiite sects. Shiites predominate in Iraq and Iran, but Iran has 4.5 million Sunnis. Sunni sect predominates elsewhere.

Until recently Gulf states traditional societies. But oil wealth undermined traditional ways; changes caused internal disruption and even revolt.

Iranian revolution. Iran under shah had close ties to U.S.; appeared stable. But shah's headlong Westernizing, his corruption and repression created enemies; Marxists, liberals, Islamic clergy united to topple shah, who fled into exile in Jan. 1979. Ayatollah Khomeini, symbol of opposition, returned triumphant as strongman of revolution. Political chaos followed. Khomeini undercut his Prime Minister Mehdi Bazargan; revolutionary committees established independent power centers; Kurds, Arabs and Azerbaijani followers of rival Ayatollah Kazem Shariat Madari rebelled against central government. At same time Islamic clergy spoke of exporting revolution.

Hostage crisis. Although Khomeini bitterly hostile to U.S., new Bazargan government moved to improve relations. But U.S. admission of shah Oct. 22, 1979 for medical treatment outraged Iran, led to fall of Bazargan government, storming of U.S. Embassy Nov. 4 by about 500 militants. They demanded shah's return, took Americans hostage.

U.S. retaliated: embargoed Iran's oil, froze its assets. UN Security Council (Dec. 4) and International Court of Justice (Dec. 15) votes called for unconditional release of hostages. Shah left U.S. Dec. 15 for exile in Panama, but no end to crisis; militants said they would only obey Khomeini.

Abolhassan Bani-Sadr elected Jan. 1980 president of Iran (second in power to Khomeini). In Feb. he and Carter agreed to UN commission to investigate Iranian grievances in exchange for release of hostages. But plan fell victim to Iran's internal power struggles. Sudden March 24 departure of shah from Panama for Egypt — one step ahead of Iran's extradition request — added to concerns about 53 hostages' eventual release.

Saudi Arabia also rocked by turmoil. In Nov. 1979 about 300 Islamic extremists seized Grand Mosque in Mecca, held off Saudi troops for 2 weeks

Bernard Pierre Wolff

in heavy fighting. At same time, Shiite supporters of Iran's Islamic revolution rioted in oil-producing Eastern Province. These 2 incidents most visible challenge yet to Saudi dynasty and its Western ties.

Afghanistan invaded Dec. 24, 1979 by 75,000 Soviet troops. Soviets apparently worried that Muslim rebels would topple Marxist pro-Soviet regime in power since April 1978. Instead Soviets themselves killed Afghan President Hafizullah Amin, installed puppet Babrak Karmal. Guerrilla war against Soviets continues.

UN Security Council resolution of Jan. 7 condemning invasion vetoed by Soviets, but General Assembly passed similar resolution Jan. 14 by 104–18 vote: called for "immediate, unconditional and total withdrawal of the foreign troops from Afghanistan." On Jan. 29, 34 Muslim foreign ministers condemned Soviets.

CARTER ADMINISTRATION POLICY

Carter Administration inherited "Nixon Doctrine." Also sought to promote human rights, restrain arms exports, curb spread of nuclear technology, especially to Pakistan. Began talks in 1977 with Soviets to "demilitarize" Indian Ocean.

But 1979–80 Iran and Afghanistan crises ended Carter initiatives; U.S.-Soviet relations plunged into deep freeze (see Issue No. 13). Presidential hopefuls accused Carter of a "failed foreign policy." Administration contended, in turn, that its policies were overtaken by events.

<u>Carter got tough</u> in Jan. 23, 1980 State of the Union address, warned that "an attempt by any outside force to gain control of the Persian Gulf region will be regarded as an assault on the vital interests of the United States of America. And such an assault will be repelled by any means necessary, including military force." To provide muscle behind the new "Carter Doctrine," Administration began plans for U.S. Rapid Deployment Force of 110,000 troops to respond to Gulf crises.

Carter also stressed need for Indian Ocean "cooperative security framework." U.S. sought rights to use military facilities in Oman, Somalia and Kenya. Saudi Arabia expressed quiet support for U.S. anti-Soviet efforts, but Pakistan balked. President Muhammad Zia ul-Haq initially rejected $400 million in U.S. aid as "peanuts."

ALTERNATIVES TO PRESENT POLICY

■ **Seek political, not military, solution to protect interests in Persian Gulf.**

Pro: (1) Two political steps would better protect U.S. interests in Persian Gulf than military solutions: effective energy program to reduce oil imports; progress on question of Palestinian rights. (2) U.S. military seizure of oil fields nigh impossible; oil production easily sabotaged. Would also stir up anti-Americanism, perhaps topple friendly regimes. (3) Military action in Gulf raises disastrous possibility of nuclear war. (4) Seeking military facilities has drawbacks: would commit U.S. to Oman's repressive sultan, Somalia's expansionist designs against Ethiopia. (5) After Vietnam, public still wary of risks to U.S. troops.

Con: (1) We must protect Persian Gulf tanker routes and oil by establishing Rapid Deployment Force, military facilities and naval presence in region. (2) We can protect vital interests in politically unstable region only by doing so ourselves. (3) Only visible U.S. military presence will deter new Soviet adventurism. (4) Friendly nations reluctant to cooperate with U.S. unless they perceive clear military commitment. (5) After Mideast crises, U.S. public newly aroused to meet global challenges.

■ **Give priority to building new alliances in Persian Gulf.**

Pro: (1) Instead of increasing U.S. military presence in region, U.S. should build up new version of Nixon Doctrine. (2) Nations newly fearful of Soviets (perhaps including Iran again) would form own defense, with U.S. supplying arms in supporting role. **(3)** Steady supply of U.S. arms only way to dissuade Pakistan and others from seeking nuclear weapons.

Con: **(1)** Regional alliance impossible without clear U.S. military commitment to assure support in crisis. **(2)** Region's countries too volatile to support stable alliance; they may use U.S. weapons against Israel — or against each other. **(3)** As in Iran under the shah, U.S. will become committed to unstable, unpopular regimes.

Select Bibliography

Hurewitz, J. C., "The Persian Gulf: After Iran's Revolution." HEADLINE Series *244. New York, Foreign Policy Association, April 1979. 64 pp. $2.00.*

Steel, Ronald, "Afghanistan Doesn't Matter." The New Republic, *Feb. 13, 1980. $1.00.*

Tucker, Robert W., "Oil and American Power: Six Years Later." Commentary, *Sept. 1979. $2.50.*

13

After Afghanistan: The U.S. and Russia

- Should we change the "rules" of détente?
- Should the U.S. accept long-term Soviet domination of Afghanistan?
- How can new "Angolas" and "Afghanistans" be prevented?
- Can we do more for human rights inside Russia?

BACKGROUND

Ever since Communists seized power in Russia in 1917, relations between U.S. and U.S.S.R. marked by periods of peaceful coexistence and even cooperation, or *détente,* alternating with periods of confrontation or cold war. With Soviet invasion of Afghanistan in Dec. 1979, détente period of 1970s appeared over, but duration of new tension unpredictable.

High-water mark of détente, when conflict temporarily subordinated to pursuit of common interests, was May 1972 summit meeting between Soviet Communist party leader Brezhnev and President Nixon. In pursuit of most basic common interest — preventing nuclear war — they signed 5-year strategic arms limitation agreements (SALT I). In vaguely worded declaration of basic principles of coexistence, 2 nations agreed to refrain from seeking "unilateral advantage," to "exercise restraint" in mutual relations. Agreed to expand bilateral cooperative scientific programs; signed trade and outer space agreements.

In key area of nuclear arms control, collaboration during Nixon-Ford Administrations led in 1974 to limited progress toward complete ban on nuclear weapon tests and Vladivostok interim agreement setting guidelines for SALT II treaty.

Détente atmosphere also paved way for 35-nation Conference on Security and Cooperation in Europe at Helsinki, 1975. West in effect accepted post-World War II territorial status quo: division of Germany, Soviet (and Polish) annexations of territory in Eastern Europe, Baltic. Soviets, in return, agreed to freer exchange of ideas, persons, and to mutual notice of "major military maneuvers." Follow-up sessions agreed on to monitor fulfillment.

Setbacks to détente. Détente began to unravel as Russians continued longstanding competition for influence, especially in third world. In 1973 U.S. complained Soviets violated "coexistence" principles by not forewarning U.S. of Egyptian attack on Israel. Soviets also encouraged other Arab nations to join war, impose oil boycott on U.S. Other Soviet actions, 1974–76, which U.S. claimed violated détente:

▶ In **Portugal,** a NATO ally, Moscow bankrolled Communists in unsuccessful struggle to gain power after right-wing dictatorship overthrown.

▶ In **Angola,** freed from Portuguese rule, Soviets sea- and air-lifted over 20,000 Cuban troops and arms to back winning faction in civil war — demonstrating new Soviet military "reach" in third world. U.S. aid to losing factions halted by Congress.

▶ In **Somalia** Soviets signed friendship treaty, built military and naval facilities. Close relationship also with left-wing regime in South Yemen.

On U.S. side, détente strained by Jackson-Vanik Amendment to U.S. trade bill, tying U.S. concessions to Soviet easing of curbs on emigration, especially of Jews. U.S. also concerned over long-term Soviet arms buildup while U.S. cutting back.

Détente during Carter Administration. Despite new strains, both sides persisted in search for strategic nuclear arms control. SALT II agreement signed by Brezhnev, Carter June 18, 1979 in Vienna. Some progress also made in talks on "mutual and balanced force reductions" in Europe and in European security review conference, Belgrade, 1977–78. Soviet Union eased restrictions on Jewish emigration: record 50,000 Jews left in 1979.

In third world, tensions persisted:

Africa. Soviet military equipment, advisers, Cuban troops in 1977 landed in Ethiopia, former friend of U.S., to support Marxist government's efforts to put down rebellion in Eritrea, Somali-backed uprising in Ogaden. As result, Somalia ejected Soviet advisers, closed naval base at Berbera, abrogated 1974 friendship treaty, drew closer to Saudi Arabia, Egypt, U.S.

Middle East. Russians, excluded by U.S. diplomacy from Egypt-Syria-Israel disengagement pacts, pushed for full-scale Geneva peace conference, co-chaired by U.S.S.R.; still excluded from peace process by Carter's personal mediation resulting in 1979 Egyptian-Israeli treaty (see Issue No. 11).

With overthrow of shah of Iran in Jan. 1979, U.S. lost one of mainstays of its policy in oil-rich Persian Gulf (see Issue No. 12). Though Soviet ability to exploit Iran chaos seems limited, U.S.S.R. retains troublemaking potential in Gulf region. Supported South Yemen in border war with North Yemen in Feb. 1979. U.S. responded by supplying arms, military technicians to North Yemen.

Asia. Détente further eroded by U.S. normalization of relations with China, Jan. 1, 1979; Soviet friendship treaty with Vietnam and support of its invasion of Cambodia, both 1978; China's 17-day invasion of northern Vietnam in Feb. 1979 following Chinese vice premier's U.S. visit; U.S. extension to China of tariff concessions and credits, still denied U.S.S.R., and military support in Jan. 1980.

U.S.-Soviet relations reached nadir with Soviet invasion of Afghanistan, Dec. 1979. Experts differ as to reasons behind invasion. Some see action as *limited and defensive*. Cite Soviet obsession with security, fear of encirclement by hostile forces (perceived U.S.-NATO decisions to deploy long-range missiles in Western Europe, increase defense budgets as Western aggression); concern that contagion of Islamic revolt would spread to own Muslim population; fear of imminent overthrow of pro-Soviet government in strategic position on Soviet southern flank; fear of possible U.S. action in Persian Gulf in response to Iran turmoil.

Others see invasion as shift to new policy of *aggressive expansionism*. First time in 35 years U.S.S.R. used its own troops in combat outside Eastern Europe. Soviets took advantage of what they perceived as U.S. weakness, vacillation, to get 1,000 miles closer to Indian Ocean, oil supply route to Persian Gulf. Their adventurism was encouraged by absence of strong U.S. reactions to 1978 pro-Soviet coup in Afghanistan itself; to Soviet-Cuban ventures in Africa; to "loss" of Iran; to Soviet brigade in Cuba; to seizure of American hostages in Teheran. Moreover, Soviets risked little: SALT II pact at seeming dead end, trade concessions and credits not forthcoming.

CARTER ADMINISTRATION POLICY

Human rights. In inaugural speech, Carter said, "Our commitment to human rights must be absolute . . . Because we are free we can never be indifferent to the fate of freedom elsewhere." Support of human rights in selected cases, including Soviet dissidents, prompted charges Administration compromised more important foreign policy interests; conversely, support called too fitful, halfhearted, low priority.

Arms control. 1977 stress on SALT and restraint gradually shifted to competitive arms buildup.

Cuba. In Aug. 1979 Administration confirmed presence of Soviet "combat brigade" in Cuba; in Sept. termed status quo "unacceptable." In Oct. nation advised of Soviet assurance personnel not assault force and had been in Cuba several years. Critics said "unacceptable" had been accepted.

Soviet invasion of Afghanistan. U.S., more than 100 other countries condemned aggression, called for withdrawal of Soviet forces. U.S. in retaliation halted Soviet fishing; embargoed grain, high technology sales; called for boycott of Moscow Olympic Games unless Soviet troops withdrawn. Also called for postponement of Senate consideration of SALT. In State of Union address, Jan. 23, 1980, President declared Soviet invasion "could pose the most serious threat to peace since the Second World War."

ALTERNATIVES TO PRESENT POLICY

■ Withhold cooperation with Soviet Union until Soviet troops leave Afghanistan.
Pro: (1) Afghanistan is crucial test of U.S. will to stand up for weak, third-world nation, victim of aggression. (2) Firm stance may suffice to convince Russians invasion a mistake.

Con: (1) Russians committed for strategic, ideological reasons to preserving puppet regime; unlikely to leave. (2) U.S. has little strategic interest in Afghanistan; should draw line in neighboring Pakistan, Iran where it *does*.

■ Suspend détente until Soviets exercise restraint in third world.
Pro: (1) Soviets' interpretation of détente permitted them to mount geopolitical offensive in third world. (2) U.S. for decade supplied U.S.S.R. computers, grain; received nothing in return. (3) Grain, technology embargoes

are strong leverage: won't cause hunger; will hurt creaking Soviet economy. **(4)** Direct U.S. pressure on Moscow is only effective deterrent.

Con: **(1)** Food should never be used as political weapon. Besides, grain embargo hurts U.S. farmers. **(2)** Embargo on high technology won't hurt Russians: in peak year 1976, only 1/8 Soviet high technology imports from U.S. **(3)** Cutoff of scientific, cultural contacts only further isolates U.S.S.R.; locks it into position of implacable hostility, dangerous to entire world. **(4)** Russians can't be deterred from exploiting opportunities in third world.

■ **Make Soviet compliance with Helsinki human rights provisos an absolute condition of détente.**

Pro: **(1)** Soviet suppression of dissent, freedom of movement, communication violates Helsinki undertakings. **(2)** Western pressure has brought the only gains, though small, to dissidents.

Con: **(1)** Rights of dissidents, emigration must be balanced with other issues in U.S.-Soviet relationship. **(2)** Best human rights approach is quiet diplomacy.

Select Bibliography

Hoffmann, Stanley, "Reflections on the Present Danger." The New York Review of Books, *March 6, 1980. $1.00.*

Podhoretz, Norman, "The Present Danger." Commentary, *March 1980. $2.50.*

Vance, Cyrus, "Afghanistan: America's Course." Current Policy *No. 144, March 3, 1980. Bureau of Public Affairs, Department of State, Washington, D.C. 20520.*

(continued from page 18)

■ Restore the draft.

Pro: (1) We need to send strong signal to Moscow of military preparedness. Return to draft inevitable anyway because of 1980 manpower needs. (2) Manpower costs, restrained through draft, make other necessary defense expenditures possible. (3) Even registration alone is necessary, says Senator Sam Nunn (D-Ga.), to cut 90 days off the time needed in crisis situation to get draftees to report for basic training.

Con: (1) Peacetime draft, form of involuntary servitude, incompatible with free society. (2) Renewed draft rests on doubtful assumption that future conflict will involve extended period of conventional warfare. (3) Senator Nunn to the contrary, Selective Service claims current "standby system" can meet manpower mobilization targets; registration not necessary.

Select Bibliography

Arms Control Today, *a monthly newsletter of the Arms Control Association, 11 Dupont Circle, N.W., Washington, D.C. 20036. Annual $20 dues ($10 students).*

"The Price of Power." Time, *Oct. 29, 1979. $1.25. Hardheaded view of defense needs.*

SALT II: Toward Security or Danger? *by the Editors of the Foreign Policy Association. New York, 1979. 32 pp. $2.00.*

State of the Union Address, *President Carter, Jan. 23, 1980.*